Getaways

Getaways with God
Youth Retreats for Any Schedule

Maryann Hakowski

Saint Mary's Press®

To Kyrie Hakowski Murawski,
my song of mercy,
may you always have the courage
to march to the beat of a different drummer.

 Genuine recycled paper with 10% post-consumer waste.
50678

The publishing team included Brian Singer-Towns, development editor;
Jonathan Goebel, cover designer; manufacturing coordinated by the
production services department of Saint Mary's Press. Produced with the
assistance of settingPace. Project staff included: Becky E. Peveler, copy
editor; Sara L. Myers, production editor; Michelle Frey, typesetter.

The acknowledgments continue on page 149

Printed in the United States of America

ISBN 978-0-88489-802-3

Library of Congress Cataloging-in-Publication Data
Hakowski, Maryann.
    Getaways with God : youth retreats for any schedule / Maryann Hakowski.
        p. cm.
Includes bibliographical references.
    ISBN 0-88489-802-4 (pbk.)
    1. Spiritual retreats for youth. 2. Church work with teenagers. I. Title.
    BV4447.H2935 2003
    269'.63—dc21

                                                2003011206

Contents

Introduction

Why Offer a Retreat?

Retreats are a special way to reach out to young people. They are proven to be effective in evangelizing and community building. They can be powerful, life-changing events for young people. They are times to get away from daily routines and include many components of a well-rounded youth ministry program and offer time to tackle issues in depth.

A retreat provides an environment for grappling with faith issues and learning new ways to pray. It is an opportunity for young people to celebrate their faith in new and different ways.

Young people and adults have a chance to share their faith-stories and build relationships of trust. Young people need and want these relationships with significant adults. Adults want to be approachable to young people and to transmit values and faith. A retreat is a place for two-way sharing of the gospel message. Often we adults learn as much as the young people do.

A retreat is a chance for everyone to have a lot of fun. We can play and pray together as one community and as one church.

An Overview of This Book

This book includes five retreats, each designed for a group of twenty-five to forty senior high young people. One-day, morning, evening, overnight, and weekend programs are offered. They cover a wide variety of topics in a way that speaks to the needs and daily experiences of young people.

One of the strengths of these retreats is that they have been improved based on feedback from teens. Youth groups and high school youth in Pennsylvania, Virginia, Illinois, and Missouri have participated in these retreats and have had the opportunity to comment on ways to improve them. In some cases, they have participated in the planning.

Another strength of these retreats is their flexibility. They can be used as written, or they can be adapted to meet particular needs of your group. Individual talks, icebreakers, and discussion activities can be used in the classroom or in the youth group setting. Many of the activities include alternate or optional activities. Some of the retreats include additional ideas at the end of the retreat that you can use to expand the retreat—for example, turning a daylong retreat into an overnight retreat. Appendix C is an index that lists all the activities and is categorized by type of activity to help you pick out those that will meet your specific needs.

The Philosophy Behind the Retreats

The retreats in this book are based on the philosophy that a healthy youth ministry program must give retreatants an opportunity to get a better sense of self, to build relationships with others, and to grow closer to God.

Developing a Better Sense of Self

Most students in senior high school are grappling with their self-identity. They are still testing their values, developing their character—deciding who they really are. Retreats offer affirmation, a chance to build self-esteem, and help identify the gifts they have to share with others.

Building Relationships with Others

Relationships—with peers and with parents or guardians—are a constant concern for young people. Retreats, by translating the Gospel of Jesus Christ into action for everyday living, can give young people options for daily decisions about relating to others.

Growing Closer to God

Adolescence is the time when young people question, struggle with, and sometimes doubt their faith. They are searching for God but often do not realize it. They are starting to discover the difference between religion and faith and are not sure where they fit in.

Retreats should offer teens a comfortable setting for examining and talking about their relationships with God. Retreats should be times to deepen those relationships and learn new ways to communicate with God.

Key Components of the Retreats

Icebreakers

These activities do much more than break the ice. They are ways to learn names, chances to stretch, games that will teach, or introductions to new segments of a retreat.

Talks

Talks are prepared by both adult and teenage team members. Teenage team members have the authority of a person speaking to their peers. Their concerns and fears, their triumphs and relationships, speak right to the place where young people are. Young people need and want to hear from caring adults too. This is an opportunity for a youth group leader, a parent, or a parish priest to share his or her thoughts and feelings and personal faith-story.

Because the speakers truly need to think about and pray about a topic before they begin writing the talk, each talk in this manual has a handout with a list of points for the presenters to consider as they prepare. In addition, appendix A has the handout, "Helpful Hints for Giving Talks."

Creative Activities

Learning through experience is a key ingredient of all the activities in this book. Variety is important. Retreat activities should challenge the imagination and offer different ways for the young people to express themselves. Some creative activities include role-plays, dramas, games that teach, videos, skits, art, affirmation, and modern music.

Discussions

As a general rule, small discussion groups should be *assigned* at the beginning of a retreat. When retreatants are asked to find their own groups, they tend to sit with their friends. If you already know the young people, assign groups before the retreat, with a good mix of quiet and outgoing members and with care to break up cliques or pairs who are likely to disrupt discussions. If you do not know the retreatants, assign them to groups randomly, perhaps breaking up cliques in that way. Some hints for leading small-group discussions are offered in appendix B handout, "Guidelines for Retreat Team Leaders."

Quiet Time

A mix of short opportunities for reflection with one longer period of quiet during retreats provides beneficial interludes. After each talk, ask the retreatants to take 5 minutes to think and reflect. On all overnight and weekend retreats, each person receives a journal and is asked to write his or her thoughts, feelings, and reactions during these quiet times. The setting for quiet time is important. Whether inside or outside, retreatants need to have room to spread out and be comfortable.

Liturgies and Prayer Services

A retreat is an ideal opportunity to expose young people to a variety of prayer experiences, to expand their personal repertoire of ways to approach God. Some possibilities for placing prayer within a retreat schedule include a morning and an evening prayer, a reconciliation service, a closing prayer, and a liturgy. Include a variety of prayer forms in your services. Music, scriptures, use of symbols, storytelling, shared prayer, mime, personal witness, secular stories or poems, traditional prayer, and prayer with motions are a few possibilities.

Eucharistic Liturgies

Often a liturgy is the high point of a retreat. A retreat, by nature, is a celebration of faith, and it is only fitting that we celebrate the Eucharist, the most precious celebration we have as Catholic Christians.

If a priest is not able to join you for the entire retreat, plan to meet with him beforehand and share the theme of the retreat so he is better able to prepare a homily. Another option is to hold your retreat liturgy at your home parish and invite family and friends to join you.

Preparation

Recruiting and Training a Retreat Team

The team approach to retreat planning allows the retreat coordinator to tap into the varied gifts and talents of several people, benefit from the perspective of both teens and adults, and share the burden of preparation.

Look for a balance of adults and young people. Try to choose adult team members who have experience with retreats. If this is not possible, invite adults who are involved with young people, active in the parish, and comfortable with their faith. Look for teens who are the natural leaders in a group, may already be in leadership roles, may be comfortable leading activities, and show a willingness to share their faith.

Some tasks for team members include the following:

- meet several times to prepare for the retreat
- lead a discussion group
- give a retreat talk
- be leaders of prayer
- participate in all activities
- give directions for activities
- enforce the retreat ground rules

Hold three to four team meetings before the retreat. Such meetings are for planning and training, and they foster community, cooperation, and teamwork. Here are possible agendas for a series of four team meetings.

First meeting

- Introduce the team.
- Explain the theme and the goals of the retreat.
- Go over the tentative schedule.
- Explain the team's responsibilities.
- Go over guidelines for working with small groups.

Second meeting

- Explain the purpose and the method of the witness talks.
- Divide responsibility for the talks and the activities.
- Discuss ways to promote the retreat.
- Designate committees for food, liturgy, promotion, and entertainment.

Third meeting

- Hold a trial run for giving directions for the retreat activities.
- Allow half the team to practice its talks, while the other half offers evaluations and suggestions.
- Plan the prayer services.

Fourth meeting

- Let the second half of the team practice its talks.
- Finalize the prayer services.
- Go over the supply lists.
- Finalize transportation plans.
- Discuss last-minute changes and questions.

Emphasize that team members are also retreatants. All team members, including the adults, are required to participate in all activities, from ice-breakers to liturgy.

Appendices A and B contain two handouts which will be useful to your team members as they prepare for the retreat: "Helpful Hints for Giving Talks" and "Guidelines for Retreat Team Leaders." Copy these and distribute them at a team meeting.

Promoting a Retreat

A great retreat is not going to go anywhere unless you promote it and get the young people in your parish or school excited about it. Here are some possible ways to publicize a retreat:

- **Personal contact:** Teen team members can call, write, or e-mail students or young people or invite them after class, at youth group, and after Mass.
- **A mailing:** Send a letter, a flyer, or a formal invitation to every young person in the parish or school, giving all the reasons for attending a retreat.
- **A presentation:** Give a presentation at a youth group or in class. Bring along young people who will share their retreat experiences.
- **A sign-up booth:** Set up a sign-up table each Sunday for several weeks. Team members can take registrations and answer questions after Mass.
- **Recruit the parents:** They are your best allies. Tell them about the retreat. Answer all their questions. Ask them to encourage their teens to attend.

Setting

Getting away from the parish or school setting is important for a retreat experience. This is preferred for daylong retreats, but it is essential for overnight and weekend experiences. Some possible settings include a retreat center, a camp, a cabin in the mountains, a shrine, or an unused convent or school building. Whatever site you consider, look for these necessities:

- adequate bathroom and shower facilities
- comfortable sleeping accommodations
- modern kitchen or a food service facility
- spacious meeting rooms—round tables are best for discussion
- recreational areas—outdoor sports courts or an open grassy area
- an informal chapel or a small, quiet room with movable furniture

You may also want to ask about the facility's group rules, the policy on damage, availability of audiovisual equipment, etc.

Permission Forms and Transportation

Check with your parish and diocesan director of youth ministry on required medical and permission forms for youth trips. Usually all teens must have a permission form and medical form. You should also have a medical form for each adult on your retreat.

Check also with your parish or diocese on regulations for transporting teens. As a rule, no one under 21 is permitted to transport teens. Under no circumstances should teens transport other teens. Make sure all the adult drivers have good directions to the retreat location. They should also swap cell phone numbers in case they need to contact one another.

Finances

Calculate what the retreat will cost. When figuring out a budget, include the cost of food, supplies, renting the facility, and transportation. Then determine the cost per person.

In most cases, retreatants must incur all or part of the cost. Some of the funds may come out of the parish budget or from the school budget. To keep costs down, you may want to ask for donations of food from parishioners or do some fund-raising. An added benefit of fund-raising is that it promotes the retreat.

Cost should not be a reason for someone to decline attending a retreat. Start a scholarship fund and make the money available when needed.

Meals

You can have the best program in the world, but if the food is poor, your retreat is going to be in trouble. If you are going to a facility where the meals are provided, here are some questions you should ask beforehand:

- At what times are the meals served? Is the staff flexible on this?
- What type of food is served? Ask for a menu of each meal you will be served while you are at the facility.
- How large are the portions? Is it possible to have seconds?
- Are provisions made for people who are on special diets?
- Are snacks provided? in the evening? during the day?

If you will be doing your own cooking but using the kitchen at the facility, you should ask the following questions:

- How large is the kitchen?
- What appliances are available?
- Do we have to bring our own utensils, pots, and dishes?
- What are the guidelines for using the kitchen?
- What happens if we break something?

Seek volunteers from the parish or school to run the kitchen at the facility and prepare the meals. It is difficult for team members, who are running activities and giving talks, to prepare the meals too. Plan meals that are filling, well balanced, and easy to prepare. Consider preparing some meals in advance and simply heat them at the retreat.

Supplies

Some general supplies are used on most retreats:

- pencils or pens
- a pencil sharpener
- white paper
- construction paper
- poster board
- glue or glue sticks
- masking tape and cellophane tape
- index cards
- scissors
- markers
- crayons
- old magazines
- candles
- copies of *The Catholic Youth Bible* (Winona, MN: Saint Mary's Press) or other Bibles
- songbooks
- liturgy supplies
- large-screen television
- VCR, DVD, and CD players, batteries
- a first-aid kit

Make a detailed list of everything you need for the entire retreat and check off things as you prepare. To help you with this, the activities in this book that require specific supplies are accompanied by a detailed list. Always bring extra, just in case.

What the Retreatants Should Bring

Give the retreatants a list of what they should bring to the retreat. For a typical retreat weekend, tell participants to bring the following: comfortable clothing appropriate for the time of year, an extra change of clothing, personal toiletries, sleeping bag, pillow, flashlight, sports equipment, and a snack to share.

You will also want to include a list of things you do not want brought to the retreat, such as boom boxes, CD players, cell phones, pagers, electronic games, and other valuables.

Emergencies

Be prepared for emergencies. Before the retreat, get the phone numbers for the nearest police station, rescue squad, and fire-fighting unit. Make sure you have the name and number of the facility's manager, especially if she or he does not live on the property. Find the fire exits so you can point them out to everyone at the start of the retreat.

Locate the hospital nearest to the facility and make sure every adult with you has the phone number and clear directions on how to get there. Make sure you have medical information for each retreatant. Record medications being used, special medical concerns, allergies, and insurance information.

The best treatment is prevention. Make sure the facility you use and the activities you choose create a safe environment for retreatants. At least one adult with you should have basic Red Cross training. Check to see if the facility has a first-aid kit. If not, then be sure you bring your own.

Discipline

Set a strict code of conduct and stick to it. Guidelines are necessary on retreat to avoid problems and make the stay enjoyable for all.

If you are on a school retreat, the school code of conduct should remain in force. Youth group leaders should meet with the pastor before the retreat to set ground rules. Also check on the rules of the facility you will be using.

Make sure all retreatants know the rules before the retreat. Go over them again upon arrival at the retreat site, answer questions, and clarify specific rules. You may want to have parents and teens sign copies of the ground rules when they register for the retreat.

Here is a partial list of retreat ground rules. You can develop other rules with your team.

1. No smoking is permitted.
2. No alcohol or drugs are permitted. Anyone bringing these substances on retreat will be asked to leave immediately.
3. Cell phones, pagers, CD players, electronic games, and other valuables should be left at home.
4. All retreatants must stay in designated retreat areas.
5. Any emergency must be reported immediately to an adult.
6. Respect and take care of the building and grounds. Any damage should be reported immediately.
7. Food is permitted only in the cafeteria or canteen.
8. Everyone is responsible for turning off the lights and turning down the heat when leaving a room.
9. Retreatants must be prompt for all activities.
10. Name tags are to be worn for all retreat activities.
11. No boys are permitted in girls' rooms, and no girls are permitted in boys' rooms.
12. A lights-out time will be in effect each night.
13. All rooms and bathrooms should be in order before you leave them.

Traditions

Traditions are fun and a special part of a retreat. They are the extra touches that one remembers or treasures for years after.

Some possible traditions are as follows:

- Ask a volunteer to say grace and allow the people who sit at that table to eat first. (You should not have any trouble getting volunteers after that meal.)
- Have everyone dress up for a candlelight dinner served by the retreat team.
- Pass out medallions, customized T-shirts, or personalized prayer books.
- Give each retreatant a reflection booklet of poems, prayers, and songs compiled by the team.
- Before the retreat, ask people at the parish or school to write words of encouragement (sometimes called **palanca**) for the retreatants. Give these either to individuals or to the group throughout the retreat.
- Pick a theme song for the retreat.
- Pick names for prayer partners to pray for during the retreat. Keep one another's identity a secret until the sign of peace at the closing liturgy.
- Take lots of photos for a retreat album. Pose for a group photo and make sure everyone gets a copy after the retreat.
- Gather with friends and family back at the parish for a noisy, joyful welcome home.

Flexibility and Prayer

After all the planning and preparation that goes into a retreat, add these two things to your retreat list:

- Be flexible.
- Pray!

Expect the unexpected. Every group, every young person, and every retreat is new and different. For that reason, it is best to mark retreat schedules "tentative." Structure is important, but you have to meet the needs and concerns of each individual or group. Be open to change and adapt your approach and your retreat when needed. Being flexible can go a long way to easing frustration.

Pray. Do it a lot. Do not let the rush of retreat planning brush this aside. Do it before, during, and after a retreat. Be open to the gifts of the Holy Spirit awakening in yourself, the team members, and the retreatants.

Center the retreat around Christ. Think of it as one long, joyous, vibrant, ever-moving, ever-growing prayer to God. Don't be afraid to let go and let God. God is what we are all about and why we do what we do.

Retreat 1

Who Are You
Waiting For?

Introduction

"Who Are You Waiting For?" is an Advent retreat that invites teens to focus on the real reason for the season, to better understand Advent as a time of waiting, and to begin discovering more about Jesus. The best time to hold this retreat is right before the start of Advent or during the first week of Advent.

This half-day retreat includes several different types of activities:

- small and large group discussions
- prayer, song, and quiet reflection
- Scripture search and poster project
- Advent action challenge

Goals

- To help the retreatants better understand the season of waiting called **Advent**
- To discover more about Jesus through the Scriptures and through the faces of others
- To make time for quiet reflection during a secular season of busyness
- To make Advent a time for bringing Jesus alive through word and action

Schedule

The following sequence for "Who Are You Waiting For?" is one way to arrange your schedule. Use the column labeled "Actual Plan" to record the activities, sequences, and starting times that will work for you.

Time	Activity Name	Activity Type	Actual Plan
8:45 A.M.	Take a Number	Group formation	_____
9:00 A.M.	Who Are You Waiting For?	Intro talk	_____
9:10 A.M.	Waiting, Waiting, Waiting	Reflection/ discussion	_____
9:25 A.M.	The Many Names of Jesus	Creative activity	_____
9:50 A.M.	Who Do the Scriptures Say That He Is?	Scripture	_____
10:15 A.M.	Break		_____
10:30 A.M.	The Faces of Jesus	Poster project	_____
11:00 A.M.	Mary, Did You Know?	Prayer	_____
11:15 A.M.	What Are You Waiting For?	Action challenge	_____
11:45 A.M.	Find Us Ready, Lord	Commissioning service	_____

Detailed Description of Activities

Take a Number (8:45 A.M.)

This exercise helps set the stage for the first two activities and serves as a way to divide teens into small groups for retreat activities.

Preparation

- Gather the following supplies:
  - ❏ tickets with numbers
  - ❏ numbered sign-in sheet
  - ❏ poster board and markers
- Borrow a number ticket dispenser similar to those found at grocery store deli counters, or make your own numbered tickets from a roll of raffle tickets. Make sure you have a ticket for each participant.
- Designate a space outside your main retreat gathering room to be the waiting room. It can be the commons or vestibule of your church or a foyer of a retreat center. Make sure there is enough room for the teens to line up.
- Make several signs to hang in the waiting room. They should say:
  - Sign in, take a number, and wait.

- Please wait until your number is called.
- Waiting Room
- What are you waiting for?

1. As teens arrive for the retreat, ask them to do the following:
   - Sign their names next to a number on the sign-in sheet.
   - Remember their numbers.
   - Get in line behind the person with the number before them.

2. When the retreat is ready to begin, call retreatants into the room one at a time and assign them to table groups based on their numbers. You could assign the first person to table one, the second person to table two, and so on. If the teens do not know each other well, you could assign the first eight to table one, the second eight to table two, until everyone is at a table.

Who Are You Waiting For? (9:00 A.M.)

This short talk introduces the theme of the retreat.

Preparation

- Recruit a team member to prepare an opening talk to introduce the theme of waiting. Or you may give this opening talk yourself as the retreat director. To help the person prepare, give him or her resource 1, "Suggestions for 'Who Are You Waiting For?' Talk." You will also want to give the presenter a copy of appendix A, "Helpful Hints for Giving Talks."

1. Welcome participants to the retreat and give any necessary directions or ground rules. Introduce the team member giving the talk.

2. Thank the team member and move on to the next activity when the talk is finished.

Waiting, Waiting, Waiting (9:10 A.M.)

This discussion helps reinforce the theme of the retreat, begins the process of sharing, and helps teens learn more about each other.

Preparation

- Gather the following supplies:
  - ❏ a copy of handout 1, "Waiting, Waiting, Waiting," for each retreatant
  - ❏ pens or pencils

1. Give the teens copies of handout 1 and pens or pencils. Ask them to complete the handout quietly, without discussing the answers with anyone just yet. When all are finished, ask each teen to partner with another teen from the same table and share individual answers to the sentence completions in the first part.

2. Ask each pair to join another pair (from their table group) so the teens are now in groups of four. Invite them to share their answers to the two questions. Encourage the retreatants to share their answers openly so they can continue the process of getting to know new people.

3. Ask the teens to hold on to their handouts until later in the retreat when they will be using the prayer on the bottom of the handout.

The Many Names of Jesus (9:25 A.M.)

This craft activity is a fun way to get teens to broaden their views of Jesus and hopefully move beyond the "baby-in-the-manger" image. It also helps to build teamwork.

Preparation

• Gather the following supplies:
  ❏ purple and pink construction paper, cut into one-half inch strips, about thirty purple and ten pink strips for every four retreatants
  ❏ staplers or cellophane tape dispensers, one for every four retreatants
  ❏ packs of thin markers, one for every four retreatants

1. Ask the retreatants to stay in the groups of four from the previous activity. Give each group forty strips of construction paper, thirty purple and ten pink, a stapler or cellophane tape dispenser, and a pack of thin markers. Have extra strips of paper available if needed by a group.

2. Introduce the activity like this:

> When I give the signal, you need to write a different name for Jesus on each strip of paper. You may not repeat a name. Fill out as many strips as you can. You can ask for more strips if you run out. When you have run out of names, staple or tape the strips together into a paper chain. They must be put together in this order: purple, purple, pink, purple. Keep repeating this pattern until you run out of strips with names on them. Are there any questions?

3. After 10 minutes, call time and instruct groups to stop working and put down all unused supplies. Ask them to count the number of names in their paper chains. Ask for a spokesperson from the group with the longest paper chain to read the names aloud to the rest of the groups. Then ask the others for any additional names not already mentioned. Lastly, connect all the paper chains together. Display the paper chain somewhere in your meeting area—you will use it again during closing prayer. Be sure to affirm their teamwork.

4. Ask: What did you learn from doing this activity? Some comments that should surface are:
   • There are many different names for Jesus and there are many ways we can approach Jesus, and call on God.

- We need to keep learning more about the life of Jesus—through reading and sharing scriptures, by going on retreat, and by attending class.

- We need to learn to relate to Jesus in different ways. For example, we can learn from Jesus, rabbi. We need forgiveness from Jesus, forgiver. We are saved by Jesus, messiah. We can talk with Jesus, friend.

- This activity required teamwork. We all contributed ideas to the success of this activity. We learned more about Jesus through each other.

When the discussion is over, ask the young people, "What is the significance of the colors and their order in the paper chain?" They should respond that they are the colors and the order of the Advent wreath candles. Close by encouraging the retreatants to call on Jesus by many names in many situations.

Note: After the retreat either display the chain in your gathering area or decorate an evergreen for the rest of Advent. If your church uses blue and pink for the liturgical colors of Advent, please change the colors of the construction paper links.

Who Do the Scriptures Say That He Is? (9:50 A.M.)

This Bible search invites teens to spend time with the Scriptures in discovering more about the person of Jesus.

Preparation

- Gather the following supplies:
  - ❏ a *Catholic* Bible for each person
  - ❏ paper and pens or pencils

1. You will want to introduce this activity in the following way:

   During our retreat so far, we have talked a little bit about Advent and waiting and we have listed many names for Jesus. This activity is a chance to get beyond the list and labels to find out, "Who is this man?" and "Who is this God?" by searching the Scriptures. Reading the Scriptures is a very important way to discover more about Jesus Christ.

2. Give all of the teens a *Catholic* Bible and instructions to find two passages about Jesus. They should record the citations and then write a sentence or two regarding what they learned about Jesus from each passage. After everyone is finished, ask them to rejoin their original group of four and share their passages and discoveries about Jesus.

3. Close by encouraging teens to spend more time with the Scriptures, not only as a way to get to know Jesus better, but to better understand their faith and as a compass to guide their lives.

Alternatives

- If the group is small or time permits, you will want to share some of its discoveries in the large group.
- If the group meets regularly and will meet again after the retreat during Advent, you might collect the Scripture citations into one handout and distribute it the next time you meet so the teens can read the passages during the remainder of Advent.

Break (10:15 A.M.)

The Faces of Jesus (10:30 A.M.)

This poster project helps retreatants begin recognizing Jesus in the faces of all who they meet.

Preparation

- Gather the following supplies:
  - ❏ poster board
  - ❏ scissors (a pair for each person)
  - ❏ letter patterns
  - ❏ magazines (ask participants and team members to bring old magazines that can be cut up)
  - ❏ glue or glue sticks
- Trace on poster board and cut out the following block letters: J, E, S, U, S. Make the letters as large as possible, using the entire poster board. If you have five groups, use the whole letters; if you have ten groups, cut each large letter in half. Do not let retreatants see the letters together or even the individual letters until later in the activity.

1. Give each small group a separate place to work on this activity. Give each teen in the group a pair of scissors along with the instructions to take out the magazines. As they work in their small groups, ask the teens to cut out faces of people from the magazines. They should search for a wide variety of faces: young, old, middle-aged; happy, sad, indifferent; African-American, Asian, Hispanic, white, and so on.

2. After the teens have been cutting awhile, give each group the poster board (or partial) letter and glue. Ask the group to create a collage of faces on the poster board, covering every part. Members may have to continue searching and cutting to make sure the entire letter is covered.

3. Bring teens, along with their poster boards, together in a large group. They should quickly discover that their letters or letter pieces spell out the name of Jesus. Ask the group: "What did you learn from doing this activity?"

Close by emphasizing that Jesus often reveals himself to us through others—those who we know well and those who might seem to be strangers, those who we can call by name and those who are "the least of my brothers." Encourage teens to be open to Jesus speaking to them through relationships with others. Advent, particularly, is a wonderful time to discover the gift in each person, not just the material gifts they want for Christmas.

Mary, Did You Know? (11:00 A.M.)

Preparation

- Gather the following supplies:
  - ❏ the song "Mary, Did You Know?" (on the CD *Michael English* [Nashville, TN: Curb Records, Inc., 1995]. This song has also been recorded by other artists.)
  - ❏ CD player
  - ❏ candles and matches
  - ❏ a copy of handout 2, "Mary, Did You Know?" Prayer Service for each participant
- Identify a chapel or prayer space in advance for this service. Have candles, matches, flowers, or any other items you typically use to create a setting for prayer.
- Ask eleven people to volunteer as readers and assign them to one of the reader parts in the prayer service.

1. Move the group to a small chapel or prayer space you have created for the retreat. Light the candles and call for silence.

2. Pass out copies of handout 2.

3. Divide the group into a left side and right side and direct the volunteers to read their parts at the appropriate times in the prayer service. Then begin the prayer service.

What Are You Waiting For? (11:15 A.M.)

This activity is designed to challenge teens to make Advent a time of action as well as waiting, to make the waiting time one for serving God and others.

Preparation

- Gather the following supplies:
  - ❏ masking tape
  - ❏ paper and pens
- Prior to the retreat, ask members of the parish staff, parish council, people involved in outreach ministries, youth group leaders, and Christian formation teachers to think of ways to make Advent more meaningful through our words and actions. Put these ideas on sheets of paper and

hang them on the walls of your meeting space. Here are just a few ideas to get you started.

- Donate food to the food pantry.
- Read the Bible every day.
- Write a thank you note to your parents.
- Baby-sit for parishioners so they can do their Christmas shopping.
- Save one dollar every day and then give to the missions.
- Pray for parishioners who are sick.
- Pray for peace every day during Advent.
- Discard a grudge and forgive someone.
- Turn the television off and really talk to your family.
- Pitch in to fill holiday food baskets for needy families.
- Donate crayons and coloring books to the pediatric ward of a local hospital.
- Send Christmas cards to military personnel deployed away from their families for the holidays.

1. Introduce this activity in the following way:

> So what are you going to do while you are waiting? Are you going to make the best of your time in line? Now that we have spent some time getting to know Jesus better, how do you think he would want us spending our time waiting?
>
> Around this room are some Advent actions suggested by the pastor, parish staff, and many other parishioners. They offer you a starting point. This retreat is also a great starting point. Study these ideas and make a commitment to at least one action that you will take during this Advent season to help prepare for the coming of Jesus Christ.

2. Give each teen a piece of paper and a pen. Invite the teens to spend some quiet time thinking and writing their personal ideas for Advent actions. Ask them to write at least one idea on their handout, but they are encouraged to write more.

Alternative

If getting input from other parishioners proves difficult due to time constraints, your retreat team can brainstorm the Advent action possibilities, or the teens can do the brainstorming as a large group at the beginning of this activity.

Find Us Ready, Lord (11:45 A.M.)

This commissioning prayer service challenges teens to take what they have learned during the retreat and make Advent a very special time of waiting this year.

Preparation

- Gather the following supplies:
  - ❏ small electric candles purchased from a dollar store, one for each retreatant
  - ❏ hymnals with an Advent song (consider the Tom Booth song "Find Us Ready," *Spirit and Song* songbook [Portland, OR: OCP Publications, 1999] no. 109)
  - ❏ the paper chain created earlier in the retreat
  - ❏ extension cord
  - ❏ the Advent prayers written by teens earlier in the retreat

1. Prepare for the closing commissioning service by teaching the retreatants the Advent song you have chosen. Ask teens—in their small groups—to choose one of their Advent prayers written at the beginning of the retreat to read during closing prayer. Light one electric candle in the center of the prayer space. Create a prayer circle around the candle using the paper chain.

Call to Prayer

As we wait for Christmas, let us pray to keep in mind the real reason for the season. Let us search for Jesus in word and deed, through the Scriptures, and in each other. In a spirit of true openness, we offer our prayers with great hope.

Opening Song

Sing the song you have chosen to begin the prayer service.

Advent Prayers

Invite half of the group to read their Advent prayers.

Shared Intentions

Invite teens to share one of their Advent actions. Rather than go around the circle, which puts pressure on teens, ask for volunteers. If teens are reluctant to start, ask a few team members to get things going.

Advent Prayers

Invite the second half of the group to read their Advent prayers.

Reflection, Candle in the Window

Read the following reflection to the group:

> A candle in the window can be a symbol of waiting, of being hopeful, of watching, or praying for a safe return. Some people light candles in windows when they wait for a loved one to come home from somewhere far away. Some light candles as a message. Some light candles as a prayer for peace.
>
> In a few moments, you will receive a candle to place in your window at home. We encourage you and your family to light it each day during Advent as a sign that you are waiting for Jesus, the Light of the World. Through your words and actions this Advent, you are waiting for the Lord with great hope.

Commissioning

Invite teens to come up two at a time and receive the electric candles from team members. Instrumental music should play quietly in the background. The team members hand the retreatants the candles saying, "Wait for the Lord with great hope."

Closing Song

Sing the song you have chosen to end the prayer service.

Alternatives

- Battery-operated candles are more expensive, but would allow you to have teens light their candles during the prayer service. You could start prayer with only a single flame lit in the dim light and end with all candles burning brightly.
- If your schedule permits, groups of teens could compose one Advent prayer using the best of their own, weaving it together for prayer. Later, the Advent prayers could be shared with the wider community.
- Ask parents to buy a candle for each teen and include them in the commissioning part of prayer.

Resource 1

Suggestions for "Who Are You Waiting For?" Talk

Use the following suggestions to create your own personalized talk on the theme of waiting. Some of the suggestions are questions for you to reflect on to come up with your own thoughts and stories. Remember, the talk isn't supposed to be very long, 10 minutes at the very most.

Beginning with Song

If you are comfortable singing or if you have a song leader for the retreat, begin your talk by having the group sing a simple refrain about waiting. One example is the refrain from "O Come, O Come, Emmanuel." Or try the Taizé chant, "Wait for the Lord" (*Taizé Songs for Prayer* [Chicago, IL: GIA Publications, 1998] no. 30). Teach whichever refrain you choose to the teens and invite them to sing it with you.

Reflections on Waiting

Use these questions as the group shares some thoughts about waiting.

- Why do we dislike waiting so much?
- How did you feel about waiting before the retreat? About waiting in line?
- We are such an impatient people. Even with so many time-saving devices, we still don't seem to have much time. What else do we hate waiting for?
- Give your own personal example—waiting in traffic, waiting in line at the store, and so on.

Advent as a Time for Waiting

- What is the church season we are celebrating?
- What is Advent all about?
- Does it get lost in the shuffle of buying Christmas gifts in our materialistic culture?
- Why does the church ask us to wait for the coming of Jesus?

How Can Waiting Be a Good Thing?

- How can waiting help us better appreciate a gift or surprise?
- How can waiting help us make a better decision?
- How can waiting teach us to be more patient with others?
- Share a personal example of when waiting was a good thing in your life.

What Are You Waiting For?

- Small children wait for Santa. As we get older we might just be waiting for the presents! Or we wait for a few weeks off from school or work. Maybe we are waiting to see relatives we haven't seen in a long time.

- Share a personal story of anticipation related to the Christmas season.

- Of course the Church didn't create the Advent season as a time to wait for Santa or presents. If we aren't waiting for Santa or presents, who are we waiting for? We are waiting for the coming of Jesus of course.

- Who is this person, Jesus? Is he the baby in the manger? Is he the man who taught and inspired so many people? Is he God, the second person of the Trinity? How can we learn more about him?

A Retreat Is a Time Set Aside to Learn More About Jesus

- On this retreat, we'll talk about Advent as a time of waiting and learn more about Jesus, the one we are really waiting for.

- You are invited to look to the manger, but also to look beyond the manger.

- Be patient; still your busyness for just this short time. Set aside all the Christmas rush worries, and hopefully, together, we'll begin to answer: "Who are you waiting for?"

- Close by inviting the group to sing again the opening refrain that you began the talk with.

Handout 1

Waiting, Waiting, Waiting

I can't wait for _____.

I hate waiting for _____.

I don't mind waiting for _____.

Wait a minute, I _____.

When I have to wait, I _____.

Last time I had to wait in line, I _____.

Who are you waiting for? _____

_____

_____

What are you waiting for? _____

_____

_____

Advent is a time of waiting. Write your prayer for Advent.

_____

_____

_____

_____

"Mary, Did You Know?" Prayer Service

Opening Song: "Mary, Did You Know?"

Leader: Let us begin in the name of the Father, Son, and Holy Spirit.

All: Amen

Left: Mary, did you know that your baby boy will one day walk on water?

Reader One: "And early in the morning he came walking toward them on the sea." (Matthew 14:25)

Right: Mary, did you know that your baby boy will save our sons and daughters?

Reader Two: Jesus said, ". . . I came not to judge . . . but save the world." (John 12:47)

All: Did you know that your baby boy has come to make you new? The child that you've delivered will soon deliver you.

Reader Three: "So if anyone is in Christ, there is a new creation; everything old has passed away; see, everything has become new!" (2 Corinthians 5:17)

Left: Mary, did you know that your baby boy would give sight to a blind man?

Reader Four: "What do you want me to do for you?" He said: "Lord, let me see again." Jesus said to him, "Receive your sight; your faith has saved you." (Luke 18:41–42)

Right: Mary, did you know that your baby boy will calm a storm with his hand?

Reader Five: And he said to them, "Why are you afraid, you of little faith?" Then he got up and rebuked the winds and the sea; and there was a dead calm. (Matthew 8:26)

Left: Did you know that your baby boy has walked where angels trod?

Reader Six: "For I have come down from heaven, not to do my own will, but the will of Him who sent me." (John 6:38)

Right: When you kiss your little baby, you've kissed the face of God.

All: The blind will see . . . the deaf shall hear. . . . The dead will live again. The lame will leap. The dumb will speak . . . the praises of the Lamb.

Reader Seven: ". . . he went about doing good and healing all who were oppressed by the devil, for God was with Him." (Acts 10:38)

Left: Mary, did you know that your baby boy is Lord of all creation?

Reader Eight: "He himself is before all things, and in Him all things hold together." (Colossians 1:17)

Right: Mary, did you know that your baby boy will one day rule the nations?

Reader Nine: The angel said to Mary, ". . . you will name him Jesus. He will be great. . . . He will reign . . . , and of His kingdom there will be no end." (Luke 1:30–33)

Left: Did you know that your baby boy is heaven's perfect Lamb?

Reader Ten: The next day he (John) saw Jesus coming toward him and declared: "Here is the Lamb of God who takes away the sins of the world!" (John 1:29)

All: This sleeping child you're holding is the Great I AM.

Reader Eleven: Jesus said, "I am the way, and the truth, and the life." (John 14:6)

(Pause for 3 to 5 minutes of quiet reflection.)

Retreat 2

Parents and Teens: Bridging the Gap

Introduction

"Parents and Teens: Bridging the Gap" is an evening retreat that invites teens to explore their relationships with their parents or guardians and ways to strengthen those relationships. Two formats are presented with different levels of parent involvement in the retreat. It can stand alone or be used as part of a larger retreat on other types of relationships in the lives of teens.

This evening retreat includes several different types of activities:

- witness talks from parents and teens
- small and large group discussions
- a look at parent-teen relationships in media
- top ten lists that challenge and affirm
- prayer with and for parents and teens

Goals

- To assure teens that they are not alone in their frustrations and struggles with their parents
- To look beyond stereotypes and clichés to the real issues facing parents and teens
- To help teens recognize that relationships with parents require hard work on both sides
- To foster better communication in building parent-teen relationships
- To help teens recognize the positive influence they have on their parents

Schedule

The following sequence for "Parents and Teens: Bridging the Gap" is just one suggestion on how to arrange your schedule. Use the column labeled "Actual Plan" to record the activities, sequences, and starting times that will work for you.

Time	Activity Name	Activity Type	Actual Plan
6:00 P.M.	Welcome and Opening Talk: Getting Along With Parents	Intro, movie clip	_____
6:15 P.M.	Why Do You Always Say That?	Icebreaker	_____
6:30 P.M.	Ten Things That Drive You Crazy About Your Parents	Journaling activity	_____
6:45 P.M.	Parents, Teens, and Comics	Discussion	
7:15 P.M.	What I Have Learned from My Parents; What I Have Learned from My Teen	Witness talk	_____
7:30 P.M.	Snack Break		_____
7:45 P.M.	Role Reversal	Role plays	_____
8:15 P.M.	Top Ten Things I Appreciate About My Parents	Journaling activity	_____
8:30 P.M.	What I Have Learned About Faith from My Parents; What I Have Learned About Faith from My Teen	Witness talk	_____
8:45 P.M.	Closing Prayer		_____

Detailed Description of Activities

Welcome and Opening Talk: Getting Along With Parents (6:00 P.M.)

Preparation

- Gather the following supplies:
  - ❏ television and VCR/DVD
- Select a 3- to 5-minute segment from a currently available movie that illustrates the tension between parents and their teenage children. The segment you use should be a common example of parent-teen relationships, so your teens will relate, at least in part, to the scene. We used a segment from the movie, *10 Things I Hate About You* (Touchstone Pictures, 1999, 97 minutes), in which one of the daughters approaches her dad and asks if she can go to the prom. His reaction, while humorous, is anything but positive.

• Ask a team member to prepare a 10-minute opening talk to introduce the theme of the retreat. Or you may give this opening talk yourself as retreat director. To help the person prepare, give him or her resource 2, "Suggestions for Opening Talk." The talk should tie in the movie with the points on the resource. You will also want to give the presenter a copy of appendix A, "Helpful Hints for Giving Talks."

1. Begin by welcoming everyone to the retreat. Share your hopes that everyone will have a good time and also grow in their understanding of how to have positive relationships with their parents. You will want to offer a short, spontaneous prayer for the guidance of the Holy Spirit.

2. Explain that to get things started you are going to show a movie segment illustrating a situation between a parent and a teen. Give whatever background is needed to put the segment in context. Ask as they watch the clip to think about their own families and how the same situation would play out.

3. When the clip is finished introduce the team member who will give the opening presentation.

Why Do You Always Say That? (6:15 P.M.)

This icebreaker acknowledges that communication between parents and teens can become predictable. Through a humorous laundry list of clichés, it reminds us that we need to go past the surface and aim for real communication.

Preparation

• Gather the following supplies:
  ❏ large white poster paper
  ❏ markers for each group
  ❏ prizes
• On newsprint make a list of common things teens say to parents and another list of common things parents say to teens. You may use some from the lists below, but add your own sayings that reflect your area of the country or the ethnic backgrounds of the families in your parish.

Parents
• If everyone jumped off a bridge, would you do it?
• When I was your age . . .
• You don't know how good you have it.
• I am not made of money, you know.
• You're not going out wearing that.
• As long as you are living under my roof . . .
• One day you will realize that I am right.

- I don't want you to make the same mistakes I did.
- Where are you going and when will you be home?

Teens

- But everyone is doing it.
- I'll finish my homework later, I promise.
- You never let me do anything.
- If you loved me, you'd trust me.
- I need some money.
- Can I borrow the car?
- Their parents let them do it.
- It's my room, and this is the way I like it.
- The music isn't that loud.

1. Ask teens to think of the most common things that parents say to teens. Give one example of your own or ask a volunteer for an example.

2. Ask teens to think of the most common things that teens say around parents. Give one example of your own or ask a volunteer for one example.

3. Give one sheet of poster paper and a pack of markers to each group. Ask them to divide the poster paper in half (vertically). At the top of one column they should write: "The Things Parents Say." At the top of the other column they should write: "The Things Teens Say." Tell them that at your signal, they are to write examples of sayings in each category.

4. Award a prize for the group that matches your list of sayings most closely. Award another prize to the group that comes up with the most examples in each category. Close by stressing the importance of communication between parents and teens and how we need to begin to listen to each other rather than just use clichés or lectures. Encourage teens to make more time to really talk to their parents or have the courage to ask their parents for time to talk.

Ten Things That Drive You Crazy About Your Parents (6:30 P.M.)

This activity shows teens that they are not alone in facing challenges in relationship with their parents.

Preparation

- Gather the following supplies:
  - ❏ pens and paper

1. Introduce this activity by acknowledging that relating to our parents can be one of the toughest relationships in life. For some, this relationship is tough some of the time, for others it can be tough all the time.

   Our relationship with our parents changes throughout our lives. It is different now than it was when we were children. It will be different again when we are young adults. And it will be different again when we are parents with our own children. Let's take a look and see what kinds of things drive us crazy about parents.

2. Give each teen a piece of paper and pen. At the top of the paper ask them to write "The Top Ten Things That Drive Me Crazy About My Parents." Allow them about 5 minutes to fill out the list on their own. Let them know ahead of time that the lists will be shared with one other person. When they are done, ask them to share their answers in pairs.

3. Close by reminding teens that they are not alone, that everyone faces ups and downs with their parents, that it is a normal part of growing up. Sometimes the people you are closest to, who have known you since the minute you were born, drive you the craziest.

Parents, Teens, and Comics (6:45 P.M.)

This activity uses the comics to identify stereotypes of parent-teen relationships. Participants begin to identify real issues that often arise in these relationships.

Preparation

- Gather the following supplies:
  - ❏ comic strips
  - ❏ discussion handout sheet
  - ❏ pens
  - ❏ small cards
  - ❏ paper lunch bag
  - ❏ flipchart

- For a few weeks before the retreat, clip a variety of comic strips from the newspaper. You should have enough so that you have at least one or two for each person attending the retreat. Look for comic strips that highlight parents and teens and the humor of their relationships. The large Sunday color comics work best, but you can also find black and white daily comics and enlarge them on a copy machine.

- Determine how many small groups of six to eight teens you will need to form. Choose a different comic strip character for each group, preferably a teen comic strip character such as Luann, Hector, Liz, Hilary, Jeremy, Alexander (Bumstead), and Cookie (Bumstead). Write the names of these characters on small cards, so that there is an equal number of each name and one card for each person attending the retreat. Put them in a brown lunch bag and mix them up.

1. Ask each teen to pick a character card out of the paper bag and write his or her name on the other side. Direct the teens to find others who picked the same comic character. The teens with the same character will form a group for the rest of the evening.

2. Give each group a set of comics and some time to look through them. Ask each group to pick one comic strip together; it could be the one that makes the group laugh the most or the one that ticks off the most group members.

3. Give each group a sheet of paper with the following questions to answer about its comic:

   • What is the point of this comic?

   • What parent-teen issue is identified?

   • Is there truth to this comic, or is it just a stereotype? Why?

   • What can we do to fight this stereotype?

   • What can be done to solve this problem?

   • What can teens learn from this comic?

   • What can parents learn from this comic?

4. After the groups have had 10 minutes or so to discuss their comics, ask a spokesperson from each group to share the group's comic and briefly report on its answers to the discussion questions with everyone. After each presentation, highlight any positive problem-solving strategies identified by the groups and write them on a chalkboard or flipchart.

5. Here are some possible insights your teens may offer. Affirm the ideas they contribute and add a few others based on this list:

   • Treat each other with respect.

   • Don't just hear with your ears; listen to each other with your heart.

   • Share your feelings and needs.

   • Talk through solutions together.

   • Learn to compromise.

   • Know when to say you are sorry.

   • Be willing to forgive.

   • Let go of grudges and move on.

   • Don't let emotions take over.

   • Think about: What would Jesus do?

   • Speak in a reasonable tone of voice.

   • Wait until you calm down to talk things over.

   • Learn to accept each other's differences.

   • Be honest with each other.

   • Spend more time together.

   • Learn to trust each other.

6. Close by pointing out that parent-teen relationships have their ups and downs, but it is important to have a sense of humor to help you through.

Alternatives

- If you don't have many comics, you can pin them all up on the wall and teens can walk around and read them as they come into the room.
- Check with your local branch of Catholic Social Services. They will likely be a resource for handouts on parent-teen relationships and workshops. You will also want to have counseling information available for parents and/or teens who might approach you after the retreat, realizing that their particular problem requires more in-depth professional help.

What I Have Learned from My Parents; What I Have Learned from My Teen (7:15 P.M.)

This talk shows that parent-teen relationships are about much more than just conflict; we actually learn a lot from each other. It also models one way to open a door to better understanding and communication.

Preparation

- Recruit a teen and parent who would be comfortable giving a talk on this retreat. You will want to ask the teen about doing this talk first! As much as possible, try to see that the teen-parent duos you choose for this talk and the second retreat talk reflect gender and ethnic diversity. For example, you will not want to have both pairs be mother and daughter combos.

  Give the teen the question: What have I learned from my parents? Give the parent the question: What have I learned from my daughter or son? To help them prepare, give them a copy of resource 3, "Suggestions for 'Parent and Teen' Talk 1." You will also want to give them a copy of appendix A, "Helpful Hints for Giving Talks." Suggest that they spend a week reflecting on and journaling their answers to the questions. After the week is over, encourage them to take some uninterrupted time to share their answers with each other. Make sure you allow plenty of time for them to work on their talk.

1. Introduce the parent and teen who are going to give the talk together. Call for the group to give them their full attention.

Snack Break (7:30 P.M.)

Consider having teens make a snack bag they can take home to their parents.

Role Reversal (7:45 P.M.)

This activity identifies sources of conflict between teens and parents. Through role-playing the activity helps shed some understanding of how to handle the situation or solve the problem.

Preparation

- Gather the following supplies:
  - ❏ index cards
  - ❏ pens

1. In their small groups, ask teens to think of situations that cause conflict between parents and teens. Ask each group to briefly describe one such situation on an index card. Check the cards to make sure there are not any duplicates. Then ask each group to quickly copy its situation on other index cards so that there are enough for all the other small groups. Distribute the cards so that each small group has a situation card from each of the other groups.

2. Ask the groups to turn over one card at a time. For each card, one teen takes the role of the parent and another the role of the teen child and role-plays the situation for at least 3 minutes. Refer them to the strategies listed on the board in the last activity and encourage them to apply some of them to the situation. After they are finished with all the situation cards, ask them to choose one situation and talk about some positive ways that they could handle the situation or solve the problem.

3. If time permits, each group could act out one role-play for the large group and share their solutions.

Close by acknowledging that all teens have conflicts with their parents, some more than others, some caused by parents, some caused by teens. Encourage teens to keep trying to work out the situation and to practice using some of the skills they learned on this retreat.

Top Ten Things I Appreciate About My Parents (8:15 P.M.)

This quiet activity reminds teens to identify and appreciate their parents' good qualities.

Preparation

- Gather the following supplies:
  - ❏ pens and paper

1. Introduce this activity by acknowledging that sometimes it seems parents zero in on our faults, instead of seeing the good we do. Sometimes we complain a lot about our parents instead of seeing their good side.

2. Give each teen a sheet of paper and a pen along with the instructions to write at the top of the paper "The Top Ten Things I Appreciate About My Parents." Give teens some time to quietly make a list of the top things they like about their parents. Some quiet music playing in the background can help create the mood.

3. When they are done, encourage them to share the list with their parents. They can talk to them about it, mail it to them, hang it on their door, etc. Do not share these answers in the large group. Some teens are self-conscious about not having two parents living at home, or might be having some real problems with one parent. Encourage teens to find opportunities to affirm their parents with their words and actions.

What I Have Learned About Faith from My Parents; What I Have Learned About Faith from My Teen (8:30 P.M.)

This talk shows that parent-teen relationships are about much more than just conflict; we actually learn a lot from each other—especially about our relationship with God and our faith.

Preparation

• Recruit a teen and parent who would be comfortable giving a talk on this retreat. You might want to ask the teen about doing this talk first!

Give the teen the question: What have I learned about my faith from my parent(s)? Give the parent the question: What have I learned about my faith from my daughter or son? To help them prepare, give them a copy of resource 4, "Suggestions for 'Parent and Teen' Talk 2." You will also want to give the presenter a copy of appendix A, "Helpful Hints for Giving Talks." Suggest that they spend a week reflecting on and journaling their answers to the questions. After the week is over, encourage them to take some uninterrupted time to share their answers with each other. Make sure you allow plenty of time for them to work on their talk.

1. Introduce the parent and teen who are going to give the talk together. Call for the group to give them their full attention.

Closing Prayer (8:45 P.M.)

Preparation

• Gather the following supplies:
  ❏ CD player and CD with chosen song
  ❏ candles, matches, and any other items to create an environment for your prayer space
  ❏ a copy of handout 3, "Closing Prayer Service," for each retreatant
  ❏ a Catholic Bible with Sirach 3:2–6, 12–14 marked

• Ask teen team members to choose a contemporary song that relates a message about parent and teen relationships. It can have a direct message such as the song "Parents Just Don't Understand" by Will Smith (on the CD *Will Smith Greatest Hits* [New York, NY: Sony, 2002]), or it can be a song you play and invite teens to think about their parents when they listen to the words.

• Ask a teen and a parent, or two teens, to prepare and practice the short dramatization "Let's Put Away the Lists" found in handout 3.

• Choose someone to prepare the Scripture reading and another to lead the prayers of petition.

- Prior to the retreat, ask the parents of the teens attending to write a prayer intended for their sons or daughters on a small sign. A prayer might read something like this: "Brian, I am praying for you. Please pray for me. Dad." Hang these throughout the chapel or prayer space so teens see them upon entering for closing prayer.

1. Move the group to your prayer space. Light the candles and pass out the prayer service handout. Call the group to silence and then begin the prayer.

Options for Prayer

- If you have additional time, invite retreatants to write their own original prayer for teens and prayer for parents.
- If you have both teens and parents attending the retreat (see alternative schedule below), you may want to conclude prayer by inviting them to share a gesture of peace.

Alternative Schedule for Parent-Teen Retreat

If you can arrange for all parents and teens to attend together, you could include parents in the retreat in the following way:

Time	Activity Name	How
6:00 P.M.	Welcome and Opening Talk, Getting Along With Parents	Together
6:15 P.M.	Why Do You Always Say That? (Do activity separately, then post lists for all to see.)	Separate
6:30 P.M.	Ten Things That Drive You Crazy About Your Parents (Parents do "Ten Things That Drive You Crazy About Your Teen.")	Separate
6:45 P.M.	Parents, Teens, and Comics (Activity is done in separate groups.)	Separate
7:15 P.M.	What I Have Learned from My Parents; What I Have Learned from My Teen	Together
7:30 P.M.	Snack Break (Teens make snack for parents.)	Together
7:45 P.M.	Role Reversal (Teens take role of parents; parents take role of teens.)	Together
8:15 P.M.	Top Ten Things I Appreciate About My Parents (Parents do list about teens; they share these later at home.)	Separate
8:30 P.M.	What I Have Learned About Faith from My Parents; What I Have Learned About Faith from My Teen	Together
8:45 P.M.	Closing Prayer	Together

Suggestions for Opening Talk

This talk is meant only to introduce the theme of the retreat, not to be an in-depth presentation on parent-teen issues. The point is to pique the participants' interest. Keep the talk no more than 10 minutes while making the following points.

Why Do Parents Drive Teens Crazy?
Why Do Teens Drive Their Parents Crazy?

- It is a common experience we all have. It is part of being a teen and being a parent.
- Part of it is a built-in conflict in the roles that parents and teens have. It is the parents' role to set boundaries to keep their children safe. It is the teens' role to push the boundaries, to explore who they are and what they can become.
- The people we love the most are often the ones who drive us the craziest. The people we live with, or who have known us all our lives (or their lives), seem to be the ones we have the toughest time relating to.
- Our relationships are different when we are children, now that we are teens, and will be different again when we are adults.
- Why do we most often take these people for granted?

Parent-Teen Relationships Take Work

- Both teens and parents need to work on their relationships.
- Teens cannot give up on their parents—even though they want to sometimes.
- Parents cannot give up on their teens—even though they want to sometimes.
- Parents are people and they make mistakes, too. We sometimes let each other down and disappoint each other.
- Parents need to learn to gradually give their teens more freedom as they prove themselves responsible. Teens need to respect the boundaries that parents set for their safety and well-being.
- Why is it hard sometimes to recognize the good and appreciate each other?

Walking in Each Other's Shoes

- What would happen if you could switch roles with your parents for one day? one week? one month?
- Would we move beyond stereotypes—to treat each other with respect as unique individuals?
- Would we begin to look beyond the conflict—to identify the causes and seek solutions?
- Would we move past a war of words—to find a better way to communicate?

Discussions During This Retreat

- How a little bit of communication can go a long way
- How we can learn from each other
- How to start working through some of the conflicts
- How comics help explore this wacky, wonderful, and worthwhile relationship for each of us

Suggestions for "Parent and Teen" Talk 1

This talk is meant to help the teens on the retreat better understand their relationships with their parents. Many teens think that their parents just boss them around and have nothing to teach them. Or they think that parents have stopped learning and growing and should never make mistakes. By presenting both the parents' and teens' sides of things you can help the teens on this retreat understand that both teens and parents learn and grow as persons because of the relationship they have with each other. We suggest the following structure for your talk with these three components. Keep your talk to 15 minutes total.

Teen: What Have I Learned from My Parent? (5 minutes)

This can include but is not limited to the following:

- Skills, values, world views, traditions, and advice about life that you learned from your mother or father. It could be something they purposely taught or something you just picked up through living together.
- Your talk can be serious and/or humorous, woven together by short stories and examples.

Parent: What Have I Learned from My Teen? (5 minutes)

This can include but is not limited to the following:

- Skills, values, world views, traditions, and advice about life that you learned from your son or daughter. It could be something he or she purposely taught you or something you learned as you strived to be a good parent.
- Your talk can be serious and/or humorous, woven together by short stories and examples.

Teen and Parent Together: What Have We Learned from Preparing This Talk? (5 minutes)

- When you shared what you were going to say with each other, what surprised you?
- What affirmed you?
- How might it change your relationship in the future?
- Close by encouraging teens—and their parents—to keep learning from each other.

Resource 4

Suggestions for "Parent and Teen" Talk 2

This talk is meant to help the teens on the retreat better understand their relationships with their parents. Many teens think that their parents just boss them around and have nothing to teach them. Or they think that parents have stopped learning and growing and should never make mistakes. By presenting both the parents' and teens' side of things you can help the teens on this retreat understand that both teens and parents learn and grow as persons because of the relationship they have with each other. We suggest the following structure for your talk with these three components. Keep your talk to 15 minutes total.

Teen: What Have I Learned About My Faith from My Parents? (5 minutes)

This can include but is not limited to the following:

- Knowing the importance of attending Mass, the need to turn to faith during tough times, the benefit of being involved in Church, and the meaning of the Sacraments.
- Your talk can be serious and/or humorous, woven together by short stories and examples.

Parent: What Have I Learned About My Faith from My Daughter or Son? (5 minutes)

This can include but is not limited to the following:

- How sharing my faith helped me understand it better, how I had to go look for answers to their questions, how their receiving the sacraments for the first time helped me renew my Baptismal promises, how their involvement in church helped me get more involved, etc.
- Your talk can be serious and/or humorous, woven together by short stories and examples.

Teen and Parent Together: What Have We Learned from Preparing This Talk? (5 minutes)

- What surprised you?
- What affirmed you?
- How has sharing faith had an impact on your relationship?
- Close by encouraging teens—and their parents—to make God a central part of all their relationships and help each other grow in faith.

Closing Prayer Service

Call to Prayer

Leader: Let us pray for all teens and parents present here today and at home. Let us pray especially for our parents and teens who might be separated from us by distance or duty. And we pray especially for all parents and teens who have died or who suffer from illness.

Opening Song

Skit Meditation: "Let's Put Away the Lists"

Mom/Dad: I've made a list of things I don't want to hear you say anymore.

But everyone's doing it.

I'll finish my homework later, I promise.

Why are you so old-fashioned?

If you loved me, you'd trust me.

You never let me do anything.

This isn't fair.

Yuck, what is this stuff?

Can we order a pizza?

You're wearing that?!

Teen: Interesting. I happen to have a list of things I don't want to hear *you* say anymore.

Oh, and if everyone jumped off a bridge, you would too?

When I was your age . . .

You don't know how good you have it.

I am not made of money, you know.

Don't be smart.

Don't be stupid.

Because I said so, that's why.

You're wearing that?!

Mom/Dad: I'll rip up my list if you rip up yours.

Teen: Done.

(Both rip up lists and hug.)

(This skit is taken from the comic strip *LUANN* by Greg Evans on September 1, 2002.)

Scripture: Sirach 3:2–6, 12–14

Prayers of Petition

All: Lord, let us be patient and kind.

Reader: Let us pray for teens and parents, that we learn to be more patient with each other.

All: Lord, let us not be jealous, or put on airs.

Reader: Let us pray for teens and parents, that we spend less time out-shouting each other.

All: Lord, let us not be snobbish or be rude.

Reader: Let us pray for teens and parents, that we treat each other with greater understanding.

All: Lord, let us not be self-seeking or prone to anger.

Reader: Let us pray for teens and parents, that we learn to place the other first and set aside our anger.

All: Lord, let us not brood over injuries.

Reader: Let us pray for teens and parents, that we let go of the grudges that keep us from forgiving.

All: Lord, let us not rejoice in what is wrong, but only in the truth.

Reader: Let us pray for teens and parents, that we will look more often for the good in each other.

All: Lord, let us remember that there is no limit to love's forbearance.

Reader: Let us pray for teens and parents, that we never give up on each other, even when things get tough.

All: Lord, let us remember that trust and hope will endure.

Reader: Let us pray for teens and parents, that we build or rebuild relationships based on trust.

All: Lord, remind us often that love never fails.

Reader: Let us pray for teens and parents, that we love each other with the same passion that you, our Lord and God, love us.

Prayer of Parents

(Parents pray this prayer together.)

Lord,

Not long ago I was a parent of children.
    Now suddenly, I am the parent of
    teenagers
and my world has changed.

So help me encourage them to be their
    own person.
When the world tells them what to wear
    and what to do,
        let me teach them what really counts.

When I try to be a friend,
    remind me that they still need me to be
    a parent.
Help me to set boundaries,
    while giving them room to grow.
Even though they aren't children anymore,
    remind me that they still need to hear
    the words, "I love you."
And in case they ever doubt me,
    let them know that like you, I will always
    love them unconditionally.

Teach me to praise them more,
    more often than I criticize.
Help me to remember that I cannot take
    back words of anger.

Keep them safe when they are not with me,
    and bless them with friends who look
    out for them.
Help them learn how to turn to you Lord,
    especially when they feel they cannot
    turn to me.

Finally God, help me learn when to hold on,
    and when to let go.
When to give them roots,
    and when to give them wings.

Amen.

Prayer of Teens

(Teens pray this prayer together.)

God,

I am young and don't know or understand
what it is like to be a parent, but it must
be very hard because so many people
are failing at it these days.

I pray for Mom and Dad, God, that
you will help them to be good parents,
strong in ways you want them to be, so I
can look up to them with admiration and
feel confident that their instruction is right.

Help me, God, when I become
stubborn and refuse to listen. Help me
accept the fact that they have wisdom
and experience because they were once
teenagers, but I have never been a
parent.

Put in my heart the respect and
consideration they deserve for their years
of hard work and sacrifice. They are
raising me the best they can. Let me not
repay them with grief or shame. Rather,
help me to give them obedience, respect,
forgiveness, and love. Most of all, God,
while I still have my parents here on
earth, help me to appreciate them and let
them know that I do! Amen.

Closing Prayer

Leader: Lord, hear our prayers as we pray for all teens and parents. We know you were a teen once. We know Mary was the parent of a teen once. You know what it is like. We ask your continued blessing on all our family relationships.

We ask this through Christ, our Lord.

All: Amen

(The data in this handout is a skit taken from the comic strip *LUANN* by Greg Evans [New York: United Feature Syndicate, Inc., September 1, 2002]. Copyright © 2002 GEC, Inc., Dist. By United Feature Syndicate, Inc. The prayer "Prayer of Teens" is written by Lindsey Krebs, Bishop Ryan High School, Minot, ND, and is taken from *More Dreams Alive,* edited by Carl Koch [Winona, MN: Saint Mary's Press, 1995], page 44. Copyright © 1995 by Saint Mary's Press. All rights reserved.)

Retreat 3

A Pilgrimage Retreat

Introduction

"A Pilgrimage Retreat" introduces the idea of "praying with your feet." Each part of the retreat takes place in a different location. As the retreatants (pilgrims) pray throughout their retreat pilgrimage, they are also called to journey in prayer throughout their lives. The themes of this pilgrimage retreat would make it an excellent Lenten experience.

This daylong retreat includes several different forms of prayer:

- music: contemporary, liturgical, and Taizé
- scripture and quiet reflection
- storytelling, poetry, and drama
- traditional prayers: Rosary, Litany of the Saints, the scrutinies
- shared prayer, journaling, and creative prayer

Goals

- To reflect on the great sacrifice of Jesus and the great hope of the Resurrection
- To encourage the pilgrims to take up their own crosses of suffering and struggle and carry them in union with Jesus
- To help teens understand the importance of turning to Jesus in time of need or trouble
- To reflect on God's immense, immeasurable, unconditional love for each one of us and to recognize that we all need to forgive and be forgiven
- To help the pilgrims work together, support each other, and light the way for each other
- To challenge teens to invite others to journey to Jesus
- To include God in all we do, including our daily lives and dreams for the future

Schedule

The following sequence for "A Pilgrimage Retreat" is just one suggestion on how to arrange your schedule. There are thirteen stops if you use the full retreat outline. You may create a shorter version of the pilgrimage by choosing fewer stops. You may also consider turning this daylong retreat into an overnight retreat starting after dinner and ending at lunchtime the next day. Use the column labeled "Actual Plan" to record the activities, sequences, and starting times that will work for you.

Time	Activity Name	Activity Type	Actual Plan
9:00 A.M.	Welcome, What Is a Pilgrimage?	Intro	_____
9:10 A.M.	"Jesus, Remember Me"	Traveling song	_____
9:20 A.M.	*The Greatest Love Story Ever Told*	Poem	_____
9:30 A.M.	Sharing Our Story	Self-disclosure talk	_____
9:45 A.M.	The Scrutinies	Prayer/song	_____
10:00 A.M.	Praying the Rosary	Traveling prayer	_____
10:10 A.M.	*Message in a Bottle*	Small-group discussion	_____
10:35 A.M.	Walking in the Light of Christ	Traveling song	_____
10:45 A.M.	Psalm 91: A Responsive Prayer	Responsive prayer	_____
10:55 A.M.	"Were You There?"	Traveling song	_____
11:10 A.M.	Finger Rosaries	Craft project	_____
11:35 A.M.	"Shepherd Me, O God"	Traveling song	_____
11:45 A.M.	*Guess How Much I Love You*	Children's story	_____
12:05 P.M.	"Litany of the Saints"	Traveling prayer	_____
12:15 P.M.	A Humble Meal	Lunch	_____
12:45 P.M.	Walking in the Light of Christ	Traveling song	_____
12:55 P.M.	What's That I See Hanging Around Your Neck?	Witness talk	_____
1:15 P.M.	"Were You There?"	Traveling song	_____
1:25 P.M.	How Music Brings Me Closer to Jesus	Reflection	_____
1:55 P.M.	Hand-in-Hand	Cooperation walk	_____
2:10 P.M.	*Tale of the Three Trees*	Story/journal time	_____
2:35 P.M.	"Jesus, Remember Me"	Traveling song	_____

2:45 P.M.	Taizé Prayer and Candle Lighting	Song/reflection
3:00 P.M.	Taizé Continues	Traveling song
3:10 P.M.	Jesus Suffers with Those Who Suffer	Newspaper prayer
3:30 P.M.	Walking in Silence	
3:40 P.M.	Waiting at the Tomb	Dramatic presentation
4:00 P.M.	End of Pilgrimage	

Detailed Description of Activities

Designate a Location

Make sure you map out the route for your pilgrimage and walk it prior to the retreat. You will need to identify thirteen different places to stop—twelve if you end at your starting location—if you use the full retreat outline. Make sure the locations are within a reasonable walking distance (5 to 10 minutes) from each other. Your pilgrimage could take place at a local or national park, a shrine, retreat center, or church camp. In an urban center, consider traveling from church to church.

Welcome, What Is a Pilgrimage? (9:00 A.M.)

This talk introduces the theme of pilgrimage and gives teens an idea of what to expect during this journey of prayer and reflection.

Preparation

- Gather the following supplies:
  - ❏ medium-size nails
  - ❏ large cross to carry throughout pilgrimage
  - ❏ a Bible marked at John 3:16 and Matt. 16:24
- Ask a team member to prepare a 5-minute opening talk to introduce the theme of the retreat. Or you may give this opening talk yourself as retreat director. To help the person prepare, give him or her resource 5, "Suggestions for Opening Talk." You will also want to give the presenter a copy of appendix A, "Helpful Hints for Giving Talks."
- Recruit two teens to read the Scripture passages, John 3:16 and Matt. 16:24.

1. As retreatants arrive for the pilgrimage, give each of them a nail to carry with them throughout the day.

2. Ask the teen you recruited to read John 3:16. Then introduce the team member who is going to give the opening talk.

3. After the talk, begin with the sign of the cross. Ask the second teen to read Matt. 16:24. Then direct the cross bearers to begin walking to the first stop.

Travel to Stop 1: "Jesus, Remember Me" (9:10 A.M.)

Preparation

- Teach the song, "Jesus, Remember Me" (*Taizé: Songs for Prayer,* 1998, no. 11) to at least three teens so they can be the song leaders for this portion of the journey. The tune is very easy to learn.

1. As the group walks to the first pilgrimage stop, have someone lead the group in singing "Jesus, Remember Me." The song leader or another pilgrimage leader may begin by sharing the special meaning of the song to them. Sing the refrain at least two times before you start walking.

2. Start by singing the refrain quietly, almost as a whisper (pianissimo in musical terms) and slowly increase the volume, then decrease the volume and end the singing as a whisper again. Try to keep the group traveling in a cluster rather than spreading out in a long, thin line. This will keep everyone singing together.

Stop 1: *The Greatest Love Story Ever Told* (9:20 A.M.)

This poem invites teens to reflect on Jesus' great love for us, far greater than any imaginable love.

Preparation

- Gather the following supplies:
  - ❏ copies of handout 4, *The Greatest Love Story Ever Told,* for each reader
- Recruit one or more readers to read the poem, *The Greatest Love Story Ever Told,* and divide up the stanzas as needed. Give the reader(s) a chance to practice in advance.

1. At this stop, *The Greatest Love Story Ever Told* should be read very meditatively to the entire group. Be sure the readers read reverently, with meaning, and loud enough for all to hear. Wait until all walkers have reached the stopping point and are quiet before starting the reading.

Travel to Stop 2: Sharing Our Story (9:30 A.M.)

Preparation

- If you feel it would be helpful to start conversation, copy the following questions onto slips of paper and make copies for the pilgrims.
  - If you wrote a book about yourself, what would it be called?
  - What is one high point in your story?
  - What is one low point in your story?
  - Who are some of the characters in your book?

- Where has most of the story taken place?
- How is Jesus part of your story?
- How do you hope the last chapter will read?

1. Introduce the walk to the next stop in the following way:

> As we share in the story of Jesus Christ today, we also share in the stories of each other. On the road to Emmaus, disciples recognized Jesus in a stranger they met and traveled with. None of us are strangers. We are only friends we haven't yet met. This is an opportunity to get to know someone, or get to know them better. It is a chance to share our story as we share the story of Jesus.

2. Ask teens to travel in pairs and only in pairs. Ask them to walk with someone they do not know. Remind friends to find other partners if they do not do as you ask right away. Remember, for them walking and talking with someone they do not know can be a bit scary. Ask them to give each pair a little room as they walk.

   If your group seems mature and extroverted, you can give it the simple directions on how to spend time disclosing and getting to know each other better during the walk. Or, you can give each pair a slip of paper with the questions above to provide more direction for sharing.

Alternatives

You could read the Scripture story of the Road to Emmaus (Luke 24:13–35) about halfway to your destination. Then ask: How have you discovered Jesus in others on your journey?

Stop 2: The Scrutinies (9:45 A.M.)

The scrutinies are special prayers celebrated during the Third, Fourth, and Fifth Sundays of Lent with adults who are preparing to be baptized at the Easter Vigil. These prayers, said or chanted, ask protection from temptation, deliverance from sin, and the courage to overcome evil in our lives.

Preparation

- Check with your liturgist on how the scrutinies are celebrated in your parish. Have copies of the scrutinies or an adaptation to use at this stop on your pilgrimage.

1. Have a retreat team member lead the group in the scrutiny prayer you have prepared. If you were unable to find the prayer, you will want to use the following adaptation of the scrutiny rite.

Leader: Let us kneel (pause). Let us pray.
All: (sing) Lord have mercy, Christ have mercy, Lord have mercy.
Or, Kyrie Eleison, Christe Eleison, Kyrie Eleison.
Leader: How were your eyes opened?   **All:** Lord have mercy.
Leader: How can a sinner perform signs like these? **All:** Lord have mercy.
Leader: Is this your son?   **All:** Lord have mercy.

Leader: How is it that he can see now?	**All:** Lord have mercy.
Leader: Do you want to become his disciples, too?	**All:** Lord have mercy.
Leader: You who are sinful, giving us lectures?	**All:** Lord have mercy.
Leader: Do you believe in the Son of Man?	**All:** Lord have mercy.
Leader: Who is he, that I may believe in him?	**All:** Lord have mercy.
Leader: You, who do not judge by appearance	**All:** Christ have mercy.
Leader: You who look into the heart	**All:** Christ have mercy.
Leader: You who have chosen us for your own	**All:** Christ have mercy.
Leader: You who bring us into the light	**All:** Christ have mercy.
Leader: You who open our eyes	**All:** Christ have mercy.
Leader: You who make the sightless see and the sighted blind	**All:** Christ have mercy.
Leader: We who judge by appearances	**All:** Lord have mercy.
Leader: We who envy the fortunate	**All:** Lord have mercy.
Leader: When we are in darkness	**All:** Lord have mercy.
Leader: When we refuse to see	**All:** Lord have mercy.
Leader: When we refuse to understand	**All:** Lord have mercy.
Leader: When we think we are all victims	**All:** Lord have mercy.
Leader: We who deny what we see	**All:** Lord have mercy.

Travel to Stop 3: Praying the Rosary (10:00 A.M.)

Preparation

- Gather the following supplies:
  - ❑ rosary beads (ask teens to bring their own, but have extras in case someone forgets)

1. Say at least one decade of the Rosary. Depending on the length of the walk, it would be best to complete the prayer.

2. Use the mysteries that reflect the season. For example, pray the sorrowful mysteries during Lent, the joyful mysteries during Advent, the luminous mysteries during the Easter season, and the glorious mysteries during Ordinary Time.

Stop 3: *Message in a Bottle* (10:10 A.M.)

This discussion invites teens to reflect on the many ways God continually reveals his love to us.

Preparation

- Gather the following supplies:
  - ❑ empty plastic soda bottles, one for every five to six pilgrims
  - ❑ paper and pens
- Copy the following discussion questions on slips of paper, then roll up the slips and insert them in empty soda bottles.
  - ❑ How does God show his love for you through the Bible?
  - ❑ How have you experienced God's love through the words of a song?

❑   How has God spoken about love through a movie you have seen?

❑   How does God reach out to you in love through other people?

❑   How does God's love come through the gifts of nature?

❑   In what other ways have you experienced God's love in your life?

1. You will want to introduce this small group discussion in the following way:

> In a movie called *Message in a Bottle,* directed by Luis Mandoki (Burbank, CA: Warner Studios, 1999), a woman finds a love letter in a bottle that a man has written to his wife who died. She is so moved by the words of devotion, that she seeks the writer hoping to capture some of that love in her own life.
>
> God communicates his love to us through many different ways—through movies, scripture, music, and other people.

2. Ask the teens to gather in groups of five or six. Give each group a bottle with the questions inside. Ask the groups to use the questions as a guide for their discussions on the way God communicates his love for us.

If teens have trouble breaking into groups, you will want to assign them to groups, perhaps by using a variety of empty soda bottles and asking what kind of soda they like.

If you have time, or want to extend this stop, you can ask for a spokes-person from each group to share some answers with the large group.

Alternatives

You may want to hide the bottles before the pilgrimage so teens have to search for the bottles before discussing God's message.

Travel to Stop 4: Walking in the Light of Christ (10:35 A.M.)

Preparation

• Teach the song, "We Are Marching" (*Spirit and Song* hymnal, OCP Publications, 2000, no. 142) to at least three teens so they can be the song leaders for this portion of your journey. The tune is very easy to learn.

1. As the group walks to the next pilgrimage stop, have song leaders lead the group in singing "We Are Marching." The song leader, or another pilgrimage leader, may begin by sharing the special meaning of the song to them. The song is simple enough that the words are not needed.

2. Try to keep the group traveling in a cluster rather than spreading out in a long, thin line. This will keep everyone singing together. For variety sing the following variations of the original verses. Repeat the verses as needed depending on the length of your walk. You can also add motions or invite your teens to make up new verses as they walk.

> We are walking . . .
> We are singing . . .
> We are sharing . . .
> We are hugging . . .

> We are giving . . .
> We are hoping . . .
> We are dancing . . .
> We are praising . . .
> We are clapping . . .

Stop 4: Psalm 91, A Responsive Prayer (10:45 A.M.)

This activity uses responsive prayer to introduce the Psalms as powerful prayers that guide us and comfort us on our pilgrimage of life.

Preparation

- Ask four teens to prepare to read the verses of Ps. 91 as indicated below.

1. Introduce the prayer at this stop in these or similar words:

> The Psalms are powerful prayers to guide us and comfort us on our pilgrimage of life. The psalms express the emotions of our relationship with God. Even though they were written so long ago, it is still easy to find ourselves in the Psalms today.
>
> There are many forms of prayer. The way we pray the Psalms at Mass—between the first and second readings—is a responsive prayer.

2. Direct the teens you have chosen to begin the prayer.

Reader 1: Our response is: "Be with me, Lord, when I am in trouble."
All: Be with me, Lord, when I am in trouble.
Reader 1: You who dwell in the shelter of the Most High,
   who abide in the shadow of the Almighty,
Say to the LORD, "My refuge and my fortress,
   my God, in whom I trust."
All: Be with me, Lord, when I am in trouble.
Reader 2: No evil shall befall you,
   nor affliction come near your tent,
For to his angels he has given a command about you,
   that they guard you in all of your ways.
All: Be with me, Lord, when I am in trouble.
Reader 3: Upon their hands they shall bear you up,
   lest you dash your foot against a stone.
You shall tread on the asp and the viper;
   you shall trample down the lion and the dragon.
All: Be with me, Lord, when I am in trouble.
Reader 4: Because he clings to me, I will deliver him;
   I will set him on high because he acknowledges my name.
He shall call upon me, and I will answer him;
   I will be with him in distress;
I will deliver him and glorify him.
All: Be with me, Lord, when I am in trouble.

(Excerpts from the *Lectionary for Mass for Use in the Dioceses of the United States of America,* second typical edition © 1998, 1997, 1970, Confraternity

Alternative

If your group likes to sing, sing the version of this psalm immortalized in "On Eagles Wings."

Travel to Stop 5: "Were You There?" (10:55 A.M.)

Preparation

- Teach the African American spiritual, "Were You There?" (*Breaking Bread 2003*, no. 160), to at least three teens so they can be the song leaders for this portion of your journey. The tune is repetitive and very easy to learn.

1. As the group walks to the next pilgrimage stop, have song leaders lead the group in singing "Were You There?" (no. 160). The song is simple enough that copy of the words is not needed. Sing the first verse two times before you start walking.

2. Try to keep the group traveling in a cluster rather than spreading out in a long, thin line. This will keep everyone singing together. As you walk sing the following variations of the original verses. Repeat the verses as needed depending on the length of your walk.

Traditional Verses

> Were you there when they nailed him to the tree?
> Were you there when they laid him in the tomb?

Station of the Cross Verses

> Were you there when He prayed "Thy will be done"?
> Were you there when Jesus was betrayed?
> Were you there when Jesus was condemned?
> Were you there when they crowned His head with thorns?
> Were you there when He took up the cross of wood?
> Were you there when the women wept for Him?
> Were you there when they crucified the Lord?
> Were you there when they laid Him in the tomb?
> Were you there when He rose and conquered death?

(This song was adapted from "Were You There?" *Breaking Bread 2003*, no. 160.)

Stop 5: Finger Rosaries (11:10 A.M.)

This craft gives teens a chance to make something as they pray. It helps them reflect on the impact Jesus has on our lives. It also serves as a keepsake to remember this pilgrimage retreat.

Preparation

- Gather the following supplies:
  - ❏ a foot-long piece of heavy string or thin cord for each person
  - ❏ a rosary crucifix for each person. The beads and string or cord can be purchased at most craft stores. The rosary crucifix can be purchased at a religious goods store. One possible mail-order source is: Our Lady's Rosary Makers, 4611 Poplar Level Road, P.O. Box 37080, Louisville, KY 40233, (502) 968-1434 or at *www.olrm.win.net/*.
  - ❏ one each of the following colors of beads for each person: white, gray, dark blue, purple, red, yellow, orange, green, light blue, and clear
  - ❏ snack-size plastic bags
  - ❏ a copy of handout 5, which explains the significance of each bead
- Make a sample of a finger rosary as described below.
- Place a piece of string, a rosary crucifix, and one of each color of bead into small snack-size plastic bags, creating one bag for each pilgrim.

1. Invite the participants to create finger rosaries by giving them the following directions:

   First, string the beads on the string in the same order that the colors are listed on the handout. Next, take the two ends of the string and thread them through the crucifix loop in opposite directions, so that one string is coming out of the right side of the loop and one string out of the left side of the loop. Knot both ends of the string, making sure the knots are large enough to keep the string from slipping through the crucifix loop.

2. When they have completed the project, invite teens to read over and reflect on the handout.

Travel to Stop 6: "Shepherd Me, O God" (11:35 A.M.)

Preparation

- Teach the song, "Shepherd Me, O God" (no. 501), to at least three teens so they can be the song leaders for this portion of your journey. You may want to have the song leaders do the verses and have everyone sing the refrain. If you want all to sing the entire song, you should provide song sheets.

1. The song leaders, or another pilgrimage leader, will begin by sharing the special meaning of the song to pilgrims. Have the song leaders teach the refrain before you start walking.

2. Try to keep the group traveling in a cluster rather than spreading out in a long, thin line. This will keep everyone singing together. Repeat the verses as needed depending on the length of your walk. You can invite your teens to add hand motions to the refrain.

Stop 6: *Guess How Much I Love You* (11:45 A.M.)

This children's tale uses the power of storytelling to remind us all of God's limitless love for each and every one of us.

Preparation

- Gather the following supplies:
  - ❏ the book *Guess How Much I Love You* (by Sam McBratney [Cambridge, MA: Candlewick Press], 1995). This is a classic children's story found in most libraries.
- Decide who is going to read the story to the group and have the person practice beforehand. Possibly, two people can read this story, one as Big Nutbrown Hare and the other as Little Nutbrown Hare. Make sure the reader(s) shows the pictures on each page to the group, as in a library's story hour for children.

1. You could introduce this activity by stressing the importance of story-telling as a form of prayer. Even Jesus loved to tell parables to help the disciples understand the Kingdom of God. Then read the book to the group.

2. After the story is finished invite the group to discuss the following questions.
   - Who does Little Nutbrown Hare remind you of?
   - Who does Big Nutbrown Hare remind you of?
   - How does Little Nutbrown Hare remind us of ourselves?
   - How does Big Nutbrown Hare remind us of God?

Travel to Stop 7: Litany of the Saints (12:05 P.M.)

Preparation

- Teach several teens how to lead a Litany of the Saints. You could use a refrain such as "Litany of the Saints" (*Breaking Bread 2003*, no. 716). Provide the song leaders with a list of saints' names to use. Perhaps include the baptismal names of all the teen pilgrims.

1. Explain the tradition of the Litany of the Saints in these or similar words:

   A litany is a form of prayer consisting of a series of prayers and responses said alternately by a prayer leader and a group. There are many different litanies in the Catholic tradition, but the Litany of the Saints is believed to be one of the oldest. This prayer is used traditionally at the Easter Vigil, at ordinations, and many other times. We, as Catholics, believe in the communion of saints, and that the saints join us more closely to Jesus through their prayer intercessions. In this prayer, we call on them to intercede to Jesus for our needs and concerns.

2. Have the song leaders teach the pilgrims the version of the Litany of the Saints you are going to use. Practice a couple of times before you begin walking so the pilgrims understand the call and response nature of this prayer. Try to keep the group traveling in a cluster. This will keep everyone singing together.

Stop 7: A Humble Meal (12:15 P.M.)

This activity reminds us of our blessings of abundance and serves as a prayer for those who have much, much less than us to eat.

Preparation

- Choose the menu for a humble meal. If your parish has a sister parish in another country—such as Haiti—you might want to eat what is considered a basic meal there. You may also want to use "Operation Rice Bowl," a Catholic Relief Services' program, as a resource in choosing a meal from a country in need.

1. Lead a meal grace as in your parish or school tradition. Include in your prayer those who have little to eat or nothing to eat this day.

2. Eat in small groups and ask the teens to serve each other. If you are serving food that reflects a sister parish or a particular country, you could ask someone to speak briefly about the parish or the country.

Travel to Stop 8: Walking in the Light of Christ (12:45 P.M.)

See 10:35 A.M. activity.

Stop 8: What's That I See Hanging Around Your Neck? (12:55 P.M.)

This talk invites teens to reflect on the real meaning of the cross and the message we send when we wear or display the cross.

Preparation

- Ask a team member to prepare a 10-minute talk on the meaning of the cross. To help the person prepare, give him or her resource 6, "Suggestions for 'Meaning of the Cross' Talk." You will also want to give the presenter a copy of appendix A, "Helpful Hints for Giving Talks." If you have several teens comfortable with giving witness talks, ask more than one to witness on how they feel when they look at Jesus on the cross.

1. Ask for the young people's attention and introduce the person who is giving the talk. After the talk has been given, allow time for people to comment or add their reflections.

Travel to Stop 9: "Were You There?" (1:15 P.M.)

See 10:55 A.M. activity.

Stop 9: How Music Brings Me Closer to Jesus (1:25 P.M.)

This activity invites teens to look at contemporary music as a means to prayer and a way to get closer to God. It also helps introduce some to contemporary Christian music.

Preparation

- Gather the following supplies:
  - ❑ a CD player with good batteries
  - ❑ CDs with the three songs the teens have chosen as directed below
- Ask three teens to choose songs that they believe bring them closer to Jesus. They can be contemporary Christian songs, secular songs, or liturgical music. Ask them to reflect on how the songs bring them closer to Jesus. If necessary listen to the songs with the teens prior to the pilgrimage to check their appropriateness and help the teens formulate their reflections.

1. Introduce this activity by talking about the power of music as prayer. Throughout the centuries, people have raised their voices in song to pray and reach out to God. Music helps us express our feelings and experiences to God. If we listen carefully, we can often hear God speaking to us in all kinds of music.

2. Ask teens to gather in their small discussion groups. Play the three songs one at a time. After each song, allow time for discussion on how the song might bring us closer to Jesus. If time permits, ask the teen who chose each song to share her or his reflection.

Alternatives

If your schedule permits, ask other group members to name songs of their own that bring them closer to Jesus. Consider continuing this activity once a month at your regular youth gathering.

Travel to Stop 10: Hand-in-Hand (1:55 P.M.)

Ask everyone on the pilgrimage to join hands and walk together in an unbroken chain to the next stop on the pilgrimage. This activity requires teamwork and cooperation. It serves as a visible sign of how we are brought together by our faith in Jesus.

Stop 10: *Tale of the Three Trees* (2:10 P.M.)

This activity uses a children's story to invite teens to try journal writing as a form of prayer.

Preparation

- Gather the following supplies:
  - ❏ the book, *Tale of the Three Trees* (retold by Angela Elwell Hunt [Colorado Springs, CO: Chariot Victor Publishing, 1999])
  - ❏ pens and paper (or journals if your group uses them)
- Ask someone on your retreat team to prepare to read the book, *Tale of the Three Trees*. The person can either read it page by page, showing the pictures as in a library story hour, or tell the story in his or her own words while showing the pictures.

1. Again, remind the group about the power of storytelling in sharing our faith. Even if we have heard a story before—from scripture or another source—each time we hear it God reveals himself a little bit more. Then ask your storyteller to share the story.

2. After the story is finished, distribute paper and pencils and ask the young people to write responses to the following questions. Use one or two sets of questions as time permits.
   - How can you share your treasure with God?
   - How do you need God to bring peace into your life?
   - How can you be someone who "points" to God?
   - What are some of your dreams for the future?
   - How do they include God? Or do they?
   - How can the love of God fulfill your dreams?
   - How can the love of God change your life?

Travel to Stop 11: "Jesus, Remember Me" (2:35 P.M.)

See 9:10 A.M. activity.

Stop 11: Taizé Prayer and Candle Lighting (2:45 P.M.)

This activity introduces teens to the beautiful mantra-style prayer songs of Taizé and invites teens to leave the darkness and walk in the light of Christ.

Preparation

- Gather the following supplies:
  - ❏ *Taizé: Songs for Prayer* (GIA Publications, 1998)
  - ❏ votive candles, one for each participant, and matches
- Recruit several song leaders to lead the six simple song refrains from *Taizé: Songs for Prayer* used below.

1. This stop consists of singing five simple song refrains from *Taizé: Songs for Prayer*. Begin by having your song leaders teach the group song refrain 1, "Our darkness is never darkness in your sight; the deepest night is clear as the day light." Repeat this refrain several times, slowly and meditatively.

Next introduce this part of the pilgrimage in these words:

> This song is sung during night prayer, and emphasizes the symbolism of light (life) in darkness. The song was created by an ecumenical Christian community in Taizé, France, to use during its daily prayer.

Then the song leaders lead song refrain 2, "Stay with me, remain here with me, watch and pray." Invite all to join in repeating the refrain.

2. The song leaders should lead the group in singing song refrain 3, "Within our darkest night, you kindle a fire that never dies away." As the group sings, pass out the votive candles so that each pilgrim has one. Light one candle and pass the light from one person's candle to another until all the candles are lit.

When all the candles are lit, the song leaders should move on and lead song refrain 4, "By your cross and all the wounds you suffered, grant us freedom in your love."

3. The song leaders should now lead song refrain 5, "Bless the Lord, my soul, and bless God's holy name. Bless the Lord, my soul, who leads me into life." As the group sings, begin walking to the next stop while holding the lit candles.

Travel to Stop 12: Taizé Continues (3:00 P.M.)

Halfway through the walk the song leaders should lead song refrain 6, "Wait for the Lord whose day is near. Wait for the Lord, keep watch, take heart."

As you arrive at the next stop on the pilgrimage, place the candles around the base of the cross.

Stop 12: Jesus Suffers with Those Who Suffer (3:10 P.M.)

This activity intertwines scripture and newspaper clippings to reflect on the suffering of Jesus and the suffering surrounding us in our world today.

Preparation

- Gather the following supplies:
  - ❑ scripture script
  - ❑ newspaper clippings
  - ❑ yellow highlighter markers
  - ❑ twelve copies of resource 7, "Scripture and Newspaper Clippings Prayer"
- Look through a week's worth of newspapers—including local, national, and international news. Clip out six distinct examples of suffering, war,

death, violence, or abuse. It is likely that you will find so many that it will be difficult to choose only six. (Highlight a few paragraphs of each, the parts that summarize the story.)

- Choose readers for each scripture passage and each newspaper clipping. Allow them to look over the material before this stop on the pilgrimage. Make sure they are clear on the order of readings.

Travel to Stop 13: Walking in Silence (3:30 P.M.)

Ask and insist that teens walk in absolute silence between these two stops. There is no talking between this point and the end of the pilgrimage.

Stop 13: Waiting at the Tomb (3:40 P.M.)

Preparation

- Gather the following supplies:
  - ❏ a simple costume for the person playing Joseph of Arimathea or Mary Magdalene, such as a robe and a sash to use as a belt
- Ask someone—a teen or adult—to memorize this speech of "Joseph of Arimathea" or "Mary Magdalene."

Joseph of Arimathea Speech

My name is Joseph. I come from a town called Arimathea. I saw the drama unfold to the bitter end. I was with the council that planned his death, and although I did not support the council's action, I wonder if I did enough. Could I have stopped them if I had been more learned or more eloquent or more impassioned in my address to them? Was I perhaps afraid of the council, afraid they might discover I was a secret disciple? Nicodemus and I were both hidden disciples, both afraid to follow him openly.

But after his death, I cared little what the council would think. Jesus warned me about the use of riches for I am indeed a rich man. I was overjoyed when he accepted me as a disciple and allowed me to use my resources to support him. That was a privilege, but not the greatest. The real privilege came when I asked Pilate for Jesus' body and buried him in a tomb meant for me. In the end, instead of burying Jesus in a pauper's grave, I had the consolation of serving him in death and unknowingly fulfilling the prophecy of Isaiah which said: "His tomb will be with the rich." I stood by when they closed the tomb. I was there on the day Jesus died for everyone, rich and poor alike. What about you? Were you there?

(Taken from *We Were There, A Way of the Cross* by Sarah A. O'Malley and Robert D. Eimer, 1996, p. 37)

Mary Magdalene Speech

I watched the life draining from Jesus—watched as he gasped for breath. Jesus had driven seven devils from me and had healed and welcomed me as a follower—me, Magdalene, a sinner, a woman.

Yes, it was my sins, my weaknesses, that helped place him on the cross. I felt that.

During the hours of his suffering, I understood what sin was—not just the sin of the Roman soldiers but my sins and every person's sins. Sin meant death; sin meant killing Jesus, my master; sin meant crucifying him to a cross. In some mysterious way, I understood what Jesus had done. He had taken my sins, our sins, and nailed them to the cross.

As I gazed at his battered body, words of forgiveness echoed in my mind: "Father, forgive them for they know not what they do." And Jesus' words of forgiveness resounded in his mother Mary's heart, too, calling her to forgive those who had killed her Son. I was present and saw the agony of Jesus. Were you there when Jesus died for our sins?

(Taken from *Journey of Decision, A Way of the Cross* by Sarah A. O'Malley and Robert D. Eimer, 1991, pp. 30–31)

1. When the pilgrims arrive at the last stop, prop the cross against a tree and gesture for everyone to sit and remain silent. During this time, the persons playing Joseph of Arimathea or playing Mary Magdalene should ready himself or herself.

2. When everyone is settled, the person playing the character should come forward and solemnly deliver his or her speech. Pause for a few moments of silence and then continue with this closing prayer.

Leader: Jesus, thank you for walking with us on this pilgrimage today. Walk with us always on our journey through life. Send us your Spirit so we have the courage to walk in your ways and announce the good news of your death and resurrection. Amen.
All: Amen.
Leader: Stay as long as you like to reflect and pray, when you are ready, place your nail at the foot of the cross and leave quietly.

End of Pilgrimage
(4:00 P.M.)

Resource 5

Suggestions for Opening Talk

This talk explains to the young people what a pilgrimage is and prepares them for what they are going to experience. Keep the talk no more than 5 or 6 minutes long as you make the following points.

What Is a Pilgrimage?

- This form of prayer is as old as our Church. Many have walked before us to pray and remember.
- Some pilgrimages in the past have lasted weeks and months. Our journey today is only for a day.
- A pilgrimage is a chance to "pray with your feet," that is, it helps us include our whole bodies in our prayer. However, we also invite you to pray with your heart. Open your heart up to Jesus as he touches your life in a special way today.
- Along our journey today, we will pray in many different ways—traditional and contemporary.
- We will pray with scripture, song, storytelling, symbols, witnessing, sharing, silence, drama, and journaling.

Why Do We Carry a Cross?

- We remember the great sacrifice Jesus made for us, dying on the cross to free us from our sins.
- We remember that we all have sin in our lives and are in need of forgiveness.
- We remember that others have wronged us and we need to offer compassion and forgiveness.
- We remember all those in our world, our country, our community, and in our midsts who are suffering from all sorts of illness and evil.
- Jesus calls us to examine our lives, confess our sinfulness, and reconcile ourselves with God and neighbor.

Directions for the Pilgrimage

- The cross leads; we follow.
- Everyone takes a turn carrying the cross.
- Be careful and watch your step and each other along the way.
- The cross is the center of all we do today.
- Let us treat the cross of Jesus Christ with reverence and respect.
- Let us treat all who we encounter today with reverence and respect.

When you finish, ask for four to six volunteers to come forward to carry the cross for the first leg of the journey.

The Greatest Love Story Ever Told

The story of Jesus
is the greatest love story ever told.

Greater than any love song,
greater than any music video,
greater than any epic movie,
greater than any romance novel.

This incredible kind of love
can't be contained in a heart-shaped box of
    candy,
in a Hallmark greeting card,
or even in a dozen roses.

We live in a society
that trivializes the word love
that reduces it to the mere physical
that uses it to sell things in ads.

Our human hearts can only imagine
the love that it took
for God to sacrifice his only Son,
for Jesus to give up His human life,
so each of us could be free from sin.

The greatest love story ever told
began in a manger in Bethlehem
    and touched the lives
    of saints and sinners
    of rebels and martyrs
    of the sick and the dying
    of believer and non-believers.

The greatest love story ever told
    is more than the life of a man
    who became one of us not only to love us
        more
    but also so we would have a glimpse at the
        heart of God
    who will never forget his love for us.

The greatest love story ever told
cannot escape the horror of the cross
    of nails driven into flesh
    of beatings and curses and abuse
    of a crown of sharp, dagger-like thorns
    and the last gasp of human life.

But this love story
    does not end on the cross.
    It does not end in a tomb.

It lives in the heart of Jesus
    risen from the dead on Easter morning.
It lives in you and me
    and in all who preach His Gospel of Love,
    in our words and actions every day.

The story of Jesus
    is our story, too,
    and we are the greatest love story ever told.

The Meaning of the Finger Rosary

First Knot: Represents when you were born.

White Bead: Represents the goodness and purity of creation.

Gray Bead: Represents the darkness and death brought by sin.

Dark Blue Bead: Represents the faithfulness of God through history.

Purple Bead: Represents the call to repentance through the prophets.

Red Bead: Represents the blood of Christ shed for forgiveness.

Yellow Bead: Represents the resurrection to new life.

Orange Bead: Represents the fire and passion of the Holy Spirit.

Green Bead: Represents the growth of the Church, the Body of Christ.

Light Blue Bead: Represents the Blessed Mother and her love.

Clear Bead: Represents the clear call to follow Jesus, to be transparent so all may see Jesus in you.

Final Knot: Represents the end of life, when every person will stand before God.

Suggestions for "Meaning of the Cross" Talk

This talk explains why the symbol of the cross is so important to Catholic Christians. Keep the talk no more than 10 minutes long. The following reflection questions and points will help you organize your talk.

Begin your talk with the sign of the Cross.

Is the Cross Present in Your Life?

Begin by seeing how the people on the pilgrimage use the cross. You might ask:

- How many people have a cross or crucifix in your room?
- How many have a necklace or a pendant with a cross?
- Do you have clothing with a cross on it?
- Have you ever thought about what it means?

Give examples of how the cross or crucifix is present in your life.

The Cross and Today's Culture

Get the participants thinking about how the cross is portrayed in popular culture.

- Give some examples of the way the cross is portrayed in magazines, advertisements, movies, and so on. Bring some magazine pictures if you can find them.
- Ask them how they've seen the cross used or abused on television, in movies, or by music stars. Ask them how it makes them feel.
- Use a poem or song to help share the true meaning of the cross.

The Meaning of the Cross

Explain that the cross has a very special meaning for Christians. While we take it for granted, for the early Christians it was a very powerful symbol that the love of God was greater than the power of evil. Think about it. The Romans used crosses for executions. So wearing a cross back then would be sort of like wearing a small electric chair today! Using the cross as a symbol of our faith is a way of saying to the forces of evil that even though you did your worst God still triumphed.

The empty cross reminds us that Christ was raised from the dead, and that we who follow Jesus will also be raised from the dead and brought into the glory of heaven. A crucifix is a particular kind of cross that also has Jesus' body. Crucifixes remind us that Jesus Christ was willing to die as a sacrifice for our sins, and that through his death our full relationship with God the Father has been restored. Catholics have a devotion to both the empty cross and the crucifix. You might bring examples of both to show.

The Cross and My Journey

Now talk about how the cross as a symbol has helped you, maybe kept you focused on God's love and the promise of heaven. Say a few words about how having the cross near you can help to guide you and inspire you in your daily life. Talk about why it is important to treat the cross with reverence and respect.

What Others Might Say

- Why do you sometimes feel funny wearing a cross?
- How have others reacted in the past?
- What can you do when the response is tough to take?

Closing

- Encourage teens to keep a crucifix on the wall of their room and to make sure they place it where they can draw strength and courage from it.
- Encourage them to keep praying about and reflecting on the cross as a way to draw closer to Jesus.
- Invite them to make the sign of the cross slowly and reverently while saying, "Do everything in the name of the Father, and of the Son, and of the Holy Spirit. Amen."

Scripture and Newspaper Clippings Prayer

Scripture 1: Luke 22:39–42

Jesus left the city and went to the Mount of Olives; and the disciples went with him. When he arrived at the place, he said to them, "Pray that you may not come into the time of trial." Then he withdrew from them about a distance of a stone's throw and knelt down and prayed: "Father if you are willing, remove this cup from me; yet not my will but yours be done."

Newspaper Clipping 1

The first newspaper clipping is read at this time.

Scripture 2: Luke 22:47–48

A crowd arrived, led by Judas, one of the 12 disciples. He came up to Jesus to kiss him. But Jesus said, "Judas, is it with a kiss that you are betraying the Son of Man?"

Newspaper Clipping 2

The second newspaper clipping is read at this time.

Scripture 3: Luke 22:54–57

They arrested Jesus and took him to the house of the high priest; Peter followed at a distance. A fire had been lit in the center of the courtyard, and Peter joined those who were sitting around it. When one of the servant girls saw him, she looked straight at him and said, "This man also was with him!" But Peter denied it, "Woman, I do not know him!"

Newspaper Clipping 3

The third newspaper clipping is read at this time.

Scripture 4: John 19:1–3

Pilate took Jesus and had him whipped. The soldiers made a crown of thorny branches and put it on his head; then they put a purple robe on him and said, "Hail, King of the Jews!" And they went up and slapped him.

Newspaper Clipping 4

The fourth newspaper clipping is read at this time.

Scripture 5: John 19:14–15

It was almost noon of the day before Passover. Pilate said to the people. "Here is your king!" They shouted back, "Away with him! Away with him! Crucify him!"

Newspaper Clipping 5

The fifth newspaper clipping is read at this time.

Scripture 6: John 19:16–18

Then Pilate handed Jesus over to be crucified. They took Jesus out, carrying his cross to Golgotha, "The place of the skull," and there they crucified him.

Newspaper Clipping 6

The sixth newspaper clipping is read at this time.

Scripture 7: Luke 23:44–46

It was 12 noon when the sun stopped shining and darkness covered the whole country and the curtain in the temple was torn in two. Jesus cried out in a loud voice, "Father! Into your hands I commend my spirit!" Then he bowed his head and died.

(The entire group should now kneel in silence.)

(The scripture readings are adapted from *The Catholic Youth Bible,* New Revised Standard Version: Catholic Edition, edited by Brian Singer-Towns [Winona, MN: Saint Mary's Press, 2000], pp. 1238, 1239, 1275, 1276, and 1241–1242, respectively. Copyright © 2000 by Saint Mary's Press. All rights reserved.)

Retreat 4

Call and Response

Introduction

"Call and Response" is an overnight retreat that invites teens to open up to God's call in their lives and addresses how they might respond. It is an ideal retreat for older teens nearing the end of their preparation for Confirmation or for teens preparing to graduate from high school.

This overnight retreat includes several different types of activities:

- witness talks
- prayer points
- reflection on scripture
- journal writing and quiet reflection
- small- and large-group discussions
- prayer services and closing liturgy

Goals
- To recognize that God often calls us through the other people in our lives
- To become more aware of the many ways God calls us, particularly through the Scriptures
- To learn more about prayer and different forms of prayer and to encourage teens to work on their prayer lives
- To recognize that there are many ways to follow God's call in our everyday lives
- To recognize both the blessings and the challenges of discipleship

Schedule

The following sequence for "Call and Response" is just one suggestion on how to arrange your schedule. Use the column labeled "Actual Plan" to record the activities, sequences, and starting times that will work for you.

Time	Activity Name	Activity Type	Actual Plan
Friday Evening			
6:30 P.M.	Arrival		_____
6:50 P.M.	Welcome, Opening Talk	Theme talk	_____
7:10 P.M.	Yes, No Candy Game	Icebreaker	_____
7:30 P.M.	Knock, Knock Jokes	Small-group formation	_____
7:40 P.M.	Stay Awake	Prayer point	_____
7:50 P.M.	Making the Most of Our Time	Small-group discussion	_____
8:20 P.M.	Snack Break		_____
8:50 P.M.	Make Time for Prayer	Prayer point	_____
9:00 P.M.	God Calls Us in Many Different Ways	Witness talks	_____
9:40 P.M.	Say Not That You Are Too Young	Journaling	_____
10:00 P.M.	The Call of the Scriptures	Scripture activity	_____
10:45 P.M.	Break		_____
11:00 P.M.	We Say Yes, Lord	Night prayer	_____
12:00 A.M.	Lights Out		_____
Saturday			
7:45 A.M.	Rising		_____
8:15 A.M.	We Are the Hands of God	Morning prayer	_____
8:30 A.M.	Breakfast		_____
9:00 A.M.	Prayer Takes Lots of Practice	Prayer point	_____
9:10 A.M.	Alphabetical Jesus	Poster project	_____
9:30 A.M.	Job Description of a Modern Disciple	Presentation	_____
10:15 A.M.	Obstacles to Discipleship	Discussion	_____
11:00 A.M.	Break		_____
11:20 A.M.	Answering God's Call in Our Work	Witness talks	_____
12:00 P.M.	The Rich Young Man	Journaling	_____

12:20 P.M.	Pray Anywhere, Anytime	Prayer point	_____
12:30 P.M.	Lunch		_____
1:15 P.M.	Supporting One Another	Prayer point	_____
1:25 P.M.	God Calls Us Through Others	Witness talks	_____
2:05 P.M.	Speak, Lord, Your Servant Is Listening	Journaling	_____
2:25 P.M.	Break		_____
2:55 P.M.	Prayer Brings Balance	Prayer point	_____
3:05 P.M.	God Calls Us Through Music	Meditation	_____
3:35 P.M.	What Is Your Net Worth?	Individual reflection	_____
4:00 P.M.	Preparation for Liturgy		_____
4:30 P.M.	Closing Liturgy		_____
5:30 P.M.	Dinner		_____

Detailed Description of Activities for Friday

Welcome, Opening Talk (6:50 P.M.)

This talk introduces the theme of the retreat and highlights the types of activities. It invites teens to be open to new experiences and God working in their lives.

Preparation

- Ask a team member to prepare a 20-minute opening talk to introduce the theme of the retreat. To help the person prepare, give him or her resource 8, "Suggestions for 'Call and Response' Talk." You will also want to give the presenter a copy of appendix A, "Helpful Hints for Giving Talks."

1. After all the retreatants arrive, welcome everyone to the retreat and introduce the retreat team. Then introduce the team member who is giving the "Call and Response" talk. After she or he is finished, review the retreat ground rules and make any needed announcements.

Yes, No Candy Game (7:10 P.M.)

This activity is an opportunity for teens to mingle and meet new people. It also challenges teens to say "yes" to learning about self, others, and God during the retreat.

Preparation

- Gather the following supplies:
  - ❏ small Tootsie Rolls or another miniature candy, enough so that each retreatant can have five or more pieces
- Choose a room or area clear of tables and chairs so retreatants can mingle and move about freely.

1. Give each person three to five miniature Tootsie Roll candies. Introduce this activity in the following way:

   > This game is called the "Yes, No Candy Game." There are two objects to the game.
   >
   > 1. To collect as many Tootsie Roll candies as possible
   >
   > 2. To not lose the Tootsie Rolls you have
   >
   > During the game, you may ask only questions that can be answered with a yes or no. Your goal is to get someone to say "yes." If you ask them a question and they say "yes" they have to give you a candy. If they say "no" they don't have to give you anything.
   > At the same time, people are going around asking you questions as well. You cannot ignore the question, you must answer, but you want to avoid saying "yes." Here is an example of how to answer a question:
   >
   > Question: Do you live in Virginia Beach?
   >
   > Answer: I moved here two years ago (instead of saying yes).

2. Give the signal to start the game and make sure everyone is participating. After about 15 minutes, or when energy seems waning, call time. Ask the group, "What did you learn from playing this game?"

3. You will want to wrap up this game in these or similar words:

   > In our daily lives, we ask and answer questions all the time. Sometimes we think before we speak; often we don't. During this game, you had to think before you answered to reach your goal— collecting candies. This retreat challenges you to think about what and who you say "yes" to in your lives. We'll give you a lot to think about in a short time. We hope you will say "yes" to learning more about yourselves, say "yes" to getting to know each other better, and say "yes" to growing closer to God.

   Have an extra bag of candy to distribute after the game so everyone has a chance to share in the treat, even though they might have "lost" at playing this game.

Knock, Knock Jokes (7:30 P.M.)

This activity groups teens into their table-discussion groups for the retreat.

Preparation

- Gather the following supplies:
  - ❏ index cards
  - ❏ pens or pencils
- Using a list of retreatants, divide the large group into small groups of six to eight people. Try to mix up the shy and rowdy young people. Make sure you have a mix of ages, gender, and ethnicity. Assign one teen team member and one adult team member to each group.
- Collect or write several knock, knock jokes. Ask team members for ideas, but make sure all are in good taste. For example: Knock, knock. Who's there? Orange. Orange who? Orange you glad you came on retreat?
- Assign a knock, knock joke to each small group. On index cards, write the knock, knock joke on one side and the person's name on the other side.

1. Give each person an index card with his or her name on one side and the knock, knock joke on the other side.

2. Direct the teens to go around the room telling the knock, knock jokes to each other until all the people with the same joke find each other and sit down at a table in a group. Let teens know that they will gather with this group whenever there is a small-group activity during the retreat.

Stay Awake (7:40 P.M.)

Prayer Point: Wake up your prayer life. Look for prayer possibilities all around you.

Preparation

- Gather the following supplies:
  - ❏ an old-fashioned wind-up alarm clock
- Wind up the alarm clock so it is ready to ring. Hide the clock so retreatants do not see it before you are ready.

1. When all the retreatants are gathered, wait until they are all quiet, then raise the alarm clock over your head and let it ring. Let it ring until it winds out.

2. You may want to make this prayer point in the following way:

   Many of us are not so fond of this wake-up call. Whether your alarm clock buzzes, rings, beeps, or plays music, it often seems to go off too soon. So we reluctantly roll out of bed or perhaps hit the snooze button for a few more minutes of shut-eye.

   I invite you to think of this retreat as a wake-up call for your prayer life. What are you doing to build your relationship with God? During our retreat, there will be many opportunities for prayer—individually and as a group—and we'll have prayer points like this one to make us think specifically about prayer.

Be open to different forms of prayer. Perhaps you never thought of an alarm clock as a symbol for prayer. If you truly are awake and aware of all around you, you will probably find prayer in all sorts of surprising places.

Prayer is both call and response. Prayer is a two-way conversation. Sometimes we do the calling on God and pray for a response. All the time, God is calling on us to come to him in prayer.

I invite you to stay awake. Don't miss a minute of the retreat. Don't hit the snooze button. You just never know how God might be calling you.

Making the Most of Our Time (7:50 P.M.)

This activity starts the small-group sharing process and helps teens articulate their goals for the retreat.

Preparation

- Gather the following supplies:
  - ❏ alarm clocks or egg timers
- Make a copy of these questions for each small group.
  - Why did you say "yes" to coming on this retreat?
  - What did you say "no" to in order to come on retreat?
  - What are you hoping to get out of this retreat?

  (Alternative Questions)
  - What relationships do you hope to form during this retreat?
  - What do you plan to put into this retreat?
  - Share one thing most people do not know about you.

1. Introduce this activity in these or similar words:

    We have a lot of great activities, talks, and prayers planned for you on this retreat. But, it is you who make the retreat what it is. We call on you and you respond.

    One of the best parts about a retreat is meeting new people and getting to know others better. This activity is called "Making the Most of Our Time." During this activity, we would like you to start sharing a little about yourself. We hope to do that all through our retreat.

    For this activity, set your alarm clock or egg timer for 3 minutes when it is your turn. You have 3 minutes to speak and answer the questions in front of you. You are to speak the entire 3 minutes. If you run out of questions, just keep telling your group a little more about yourself.

    Make sure you reset the timer for each person. And do not break the time limit. It is important to hear from each person in your group.

2. Signal the groups to begin sharing. Keep track of the time and give a 10-minute warning. If time permits, you may want to have the small groups share their answers to the question, "What are you hoping to get out of this retreat?" with the entire group. Close the activity by encouraging teens to be open to sharing throughout the retreat.

Snack Break (8:20 P.M.)

Make Time for Prayer (8:50 P.M.)

Prayer Point: It is possible to find time for prayer even in the midst of our crazy, hectic lives. Prayer can transform our lives.

Preparation

- Gather the following supplies:
  - ❏ a large, clear glass
  - ❏ a clear pitcher of water
  - ❏ colorful sponges
- Cut up dry sponges into small pieces and make sure you have enough pieces to fill up the large glass right to the brim and perhaps even above.

1. Put the empty clear glass on a table where all retreatants can see it. Scatter the pieces of sponge around the glass. Have the pitcher of water ready nearby.

2. Start by asking the group, "What are some of the things that fill up your life? What are some of the things that keep you busy?" As you call on teens for answers, invite them to place one piece of sponge in the glass for each activity they list. Some possible answers are shopping, sports, homework, studying for tests, part-time job, the Internet, talking on the phone, doing chores, practicing with the band, and so on.

3. When the glass is full and all the sponges are used up, ask, "Is this glass pretty full?" They will usually say "yes." Continue by saying, "The glass is quite full, yet when I take this pitcher and start pouring water into the glass, I can still get quite a bit of water into this glass." As you say this, pour water into the glass.

   Then ask the group, "How is the glass like our everyday lives? How is prayer a lot like the water?" Some possible answers might be:

   - We can find time for prayer in between all the activities in our lives.
   - We can always find time for prayer if we try.
   - Just as the water makes the sponges soft and bigger, prayer can transform our lives. (This activity is adapted from the "Sponge Reflection," *Vine & Branches,* pp. 44–45.)

God Calls Us in Many Different Ways (9:00 P.M.)

Teens are invited to share in the faith stories of two people who live out God's call as a priest, sister, lay minister, single person, or married person.

Preparation

- For this part of the retreat, you will need to invite two or three people to share their vocational call with the retreatants. Minimally, invite one person who answers God's call as a priest or a religious sister or brother and invite another person who answers God's call as a married layperson or a single layperson. You may also want to include someone who answers God's call as a lay ecclesial minister, such as the parish youth minister or director of religious education. If possible, invite people already familiar to the teens attending the retreat.

  To help the speakers prepare, give each a copy of resource 9, "Suggestions for Vocational Talk." You will also want to give the presenter a copy of appendix A, "Helpful Hints for Giving Talks." Be clear that they have only 15 minutes each if there are two speakers or 10 minutes if there are three speakers.

1. Introduce your speakers. Mention that God's call is closely related to our vocation in life and that these speakers are here to talk about how they have been called to their vocation as a priest, sister, brother, married, or single person. Even though there are only two or three speakers for this session, make sure you mention the other vocational areas.

2. Decide which is better, to have the speakers talk first and then allow time for questions, or to allow questions after each speaker is finished. Thank the speakers for their time and the way they gave witness to God's love through their vocation when you are finished.

Say Not That You Are Too Young (9:40 P.M.)

This activity invites teens to spend quiet time exploring and writing about the call of a person of Scripture—Jeremiah.

Preparation

- Gather the following supplies:
  - ❏ journals, one for each retreatant
  - ❏ pens or pencils
  - ❏ a Catholic Bible for each retreatant
- Make a copy of these journaling directions for each participant:

"Say Not That You Are Too Young" Journaling Directions

1. Read Jeremiah 1:4–10 again on your own.

2. Close your eyes and reflect quietly on the passage.

3. Read the Scripture passage again.

4. Answer the following questions in your journal:
   - God told Jeremiah that he knew him even before he was born and gave him a mission. How does it make you feel to know God called you even before you were born?
   - When God called, Jeremiah said, "Who me?" and God said, "Yes, you!" Jeremiah said he is too young to be a prophet. What excuses do you use to avoid answering God's call?
   - The Lord reached out and touched Jeremiah's mouth and helped him form the words he needed. How do you need God's help in sharing your faith?

1. Gather teens together and ask one of them to proclaim Jer. 1:4–10, the call of Jeremiah. Hand out the journaling directions, journals, and pens or pencils. Explain the journaling directions and make sure there aren't any questions.

2. Ask teens to find a quiet place for themselves. You can ask them to spread out inside or find a tree to sit under outside. They need to have plenty of space so they are not distracted and so they are not tempted to have a conversation with anyone other than God. Tell them that they will have 15 minutes of private time to do their reflecting and journaling.

3. When the time has passed gather the group together. Emphasize the importance of keeping journal notations private. Invite the retreatants to continue writing in their journals throughout the retreat.

The Call of the Scriptures (10:00 P.M.)

This activity invites teens to meet people in the Scriptures who hear God's call and respond to God. It asks them to reflect on how God calls them through scripture passage.

Preparation

- Gather the following supplies:
  - ❏ a Catholic Bible for each participant
  - ❏ a pad of ruled paper
  - ❏ pens or pencils

1. Introduce this activity by pointing out that the Scriptures are filled with stories about the call of God and how people respond to God. God the Father and his son Jesus called many different people in many different ways in both the Hebrew Scriptures and Christian Scriptures. We can learn a lot about call and response by spending time with the Scriptures.

2. Ask teens to meet in their small groups. Make sure everyone has a Bible and each small group is assigned one of these biblical people and passages.
   - Moses—Exod. 3:1–14
   - Jonah—Jon. 1 and 2

- Zaccheus—Luke 19:1–10
- Paul—Acts 9:1–22
- Mary Magdalene—John 20:1–18
- Mary and Martha—John 12:1–8
- Matthew—Matt. 9:9–13
- The Woman at the Well—John 4:7–15

    Ask them to read the Scripture passage and discuss the following questions:

- How did God call this person in the Scripture?
- How is God calling us in the Scripture?
- How is God calling to you in this Scripture?

3. When the small groups finish their discussions, ask a spokesperson from each group to read the Scripture passage and share the group's answers to the first two questions. Close this activity by encouraging teens to spend more time reading the Scriptures and to reflect on the Scriptures they hear proclaimed at weekend liturgy. The Scriptures were written for each one of us. We are each called through God's word in the Scriptures and we each respond in our own way. Remind them: "You won't hear God calling you through scripture if you don't take time to read the Bible."

Break (10:45 P.M.)

We Say Yes, Lord (11:00 P.M.)

This prayer service uses movie clips to raise up Mary as a model of prayer.

Preparation

- Gather the following supplies:
  - ❑ *Jesus of Nazareth* movie (RAI/ITC Entertainment LTD, 1977, 382 minutes), first part
  - ❑ television and VCR/DVD
  - ❑ a copy of handout 6, "The 'Magnificat' Prayer," for each retreatant
  - ❑ music for "Holy Is His Name" by John Michael Talbot (*Spirit and Song*, OCP Publications, 2000, no. 95)
- Be ready to play two segments from the movie. The first segment is when Mary is betrothed to Joseph and an angel visits her to tell her she will be the mother of God. It is found at approximately 9 minutes and 30 seconds into the tape and ends at about 15 minutes and 30 seconds on the tape. The second clip is when Mary visits her cousin Elizabeth and she prays what we now call the "Magnificat." It starts at about 19:12 into the tape and ends at about 21:00 on the tape. You can cue the movie so you are ready to play the first clip, but you will need to fast forward to the second clip during the prayer service.

Call to Prayer

Begin the prayer with these words or with your own spontaneous prayer:

> Mary gave birth to Jesus Christ in order to share Him with the world. She was open completely to the call of the Spirit. We are inspired by Mary, Our Mother, to serve God and to serve others. She calls us, also, to say "yes" to God's call. Let us pray for the courage to say "yes" to God with our entire life.

Mary Says "Yes" to God

Show the first movie clip in which Mary says "yes" to being the Mother of Jesus, the Mother of God. When it is finished, ask the retreatants to silently reflect on these questions:

- Why did Mary say "yes" to God?
- How can you say "yes" to God in your life?

After a few minutes of silent reflection, show the second movie clip in which Mary visits her cousin Elizabeth and prays what we now call the "Magnificat."

The "Magnificat"

Hand out "The 'Magnificat' Prayer." Divide the group into right and left sides and lead them in praying the prayer together.

Closing Song

"Holy Is His Name" by John Michael Talbot (*Spirit and Song,* no. 95).

Lights Out
(12:00 A.M.)

Detailed Description of Activities for Saturday

Rising (7:45 A.M.)

We Are the Hands of God (8:15 A.M.)

Preparation

- Gather the following supplies:
    - ❏ copies of the first and second readings of this prayer service
    - ❏ an optional shared reflection sheet
- Ask two teens the night before to read the first and second readings.

Call to Prayer

Begin the prayer with these or similar words:

> Let us pray, as we begin this day, that we recognize Christ in ourselves and others. May we recognize the often quoted truth that Jesus has no hands and feet but ours.

First Reading

Reader 1: A reading inspired by the Gospel of Mark.
Some people brought teenagers to Jesus for him to place his hands on them. But some of the other adults in the parish scolded the people. "Send the teens away," they said.

> . . . they'll just mess up the parish hall.
> . . . they'll goof around during Mass.
> . . . they won't wear the right clothes to church.
> . . . they'll play their loud music wherever they go.
> . . . they'll use up all the money in the parish budget.
> . . . they'll drop chip and pretzel crumbs all over our new kitchen.
> . . . they would rather go to the mall anyway.

Just forget about them until they are adults and know how to act.

When Jesus heard this, he was angry and said to the parishioners: "Let the teenagers come to me and do not stop them, because the Kingdom of God belongs to such as these. I assure you that whoever does not receive the kingdom of God as a teenager, will never enter it." Then he took the teenagers in his arms, placed his hands on each of them, and blessed them.

(When the reading is finished, allow some time for quiet reflection.)

Second Reading

Reader 2: This prayer was written by a high school student, Mandy White.

> People who you can trust
>   are hard to find.
> People who care about you
>   are hard to find.
> People who can help you
>   are hard to find.
> People who like you for you
>   are hard to find.
> People just like you
>   are hard to find.

(Prayer is by Mandy White from *Dreams Alive: Prayers by Teenagers,* Saint Mary's Press, 1991, p. 30.)

Shared Prayer

Leader: Please repeat my words and actions.
Lord, help these hands be hands of comfort.
>   (Put hand on shoulder of person next to you.)

Lord, help us lift these hands in prayer.
>   (Fold hands in prayer.)

Lord, help us use these hands to serve.
>   (Cup hands and extend outward.)

Lord, help us use these hands to celebrate.
> (Raise hands above head.)

Lord, help us extend these hands in invitation.
> (Extend one hand out.)

Lord, help us join our hands in community.
> (Join hands in a circle.)

Leader: Loving Father, we place our hands in yours. As we reflect on your call and our response, let us never forget that we are the hands of Jesus. Bless us and all who we touch today and every day.

All: Amen

Breakfast (8:30 A.M.)

Prayer Takes Lots of Practice (9:00 A.M.)

Prayer Point: The more you pray the more comfortable you become with it. The more you pray, the better you become at praying.

Preparation

- Gather the following supplies:
  - ❏ a basketball and a basketball hoop, or a hockey stick, a hockey puck, and a goal
- Ideally the site of your retreat has an indoor or outdoor basketball hoop or has a large space where you can shoot a few hockey goals. If not, use a soft foam ball and a hoop for indoors.

1. Have everyone gather at the basketball hoop or near the hockey goal. Invite teens to take a few turns shooting some hoops or shooting goals. Encourage everyone to take a turn, even those who say they don't know how to play basketball or that they aren't too good at it.

2. Ask the group, "What can basketball, or for that matter any sport, teach us about prayer?"

    Summarize their answers by stressing that just as excelling at sports requires practice, excelling at prayer requires practice also. Yes, prayer comes easier to some. But many of the great masters of prayer in our Catholic tradition often wrote that prayer requires practice. The more we pray, the more we will become comfortable with praying.

    We can do this by:

    - choosing a consistent time and space to pray;
    - finding opportunities to pray throughout our day;
    - praying every morning or evening (depending on when we feel our best);
    - finding time to pray alone, but also praying with our community—especially at weekend liturgy.

Alphabetical Jesus (9:10 A.M.)

This activity uses qualities of Jesus as a springboard to discuss the qualities needed to answer Jesus' call to be disciples.

Preparation

- Gather the following supplies:
  - ❏ poster paper
  - ❏ markers

1. Start by giving each small group a pack of markers and a large piece of poster paper. Ask one person from each group to write the letters of the alphabet vertically on the left side of the poster paper.

2. Introduce this activity in the following way:

> We will be spending a good part of our morning talking about the call of the disciples, what qualifications are needed to be a modern disciple, and what gets in the way of trying to be a disciple. But let's look first at this person, Jesus, who is doing the calling. Perhaps if we learn more about him, we'll learn more about what it takes to follow him.
>
> For each letter on your paper, your group is to work together to identify a word or a phrase to describe Jesus. After the list is complete, go through it and put an "S" next to the words that describe a servant or someone who serves. Put an "L" next to words that describe someone who leads. Pick three words that you think best describe Jesus—and tell the people in your group why.

3. When the groups have finished ask the entire group, "What have you learned about Jesus from this activity? What have you learned about a call to follow Jesus from this activity?"

Job Description of a Modern Disciple (9:30 A.M.)

This activity illustrates that there is no such thing as a perfect disciple. We each have what it takes to answer Jesus' call in our own way.

Preparation

- Gather the following supplies:
  - ❏ a variety of supplies for making different kinds of presentations, poster board, markers, pencils, papers, and so on

1. Introduce this activity in the following way, addressing the small groups:

> You work for a job placement company. You match the right people with the right jobs. One day, Jesus walks into your office. He wants to do some recruiting for disciples and would like to have a more updated job description. He'll be back in 10 minutes to see what you have come up with. You can choose how you would like to make the presentation—to Jesus—and to the rest of us. You can create a newspaper ad, a resume, a job description, a Web site, a billboard, or a wanted poster.

2. When the 10 minutes are up, ask each group to make their presentation. Draw together the responses, identifying similarities and differences. Then ask the group, "Can anyone fit your job description? Can even the twelve Apostles fit your job description?"

3. Read one of the qualifications Jesus gave in Scripture: "You shall love the Lord your God with all your heart, and with all your soul, and with all your mind. . . . You shall love your neighbor as yourself" (Matt. 22:37; 22:39). Then ask them: "What have you learned about what it takes to answer Jesus' call from this activity?"

4. Close by thanking teens for their creativity and great ideas. Emphasize that Jesus' call is for each of us, that we all have unique gifts and talents to answer God's call.

Obstacles to Discipleship (10:15 A.M.)

This activity acknowledges the many obstacles that face disciples of Jesus and begins a discussion on ways to overcome these obstacles.

Preparation

- Gather the following supplies:
  - ❏ bright orange safety cones, one for each small group
  - ❏ sticky notes, enough so each participant has at least two
  - ❏ pens or pencils

1. Distribute pencils or pens to each person and give each group a pack of sticky notes. Place a bright orange safety cone in the center of each small group. Introduce the activity like this:

   Okay, so we have our job descriptions—the ones we wrote, the qualities of Jesus, and the example found in Scriptures—but it just isn't that easy.
   There are a lot of obstacles that get in the way of being a disciple of Jesus—especially in today's day and age. I'd like you to think about what some of those obstacles are and write two obstacles on two sticky notes. Then come and place your sticky notes on the orange cone in the center of your small group. Please do this in silence.

2. When each group is finished, continue:

   Now I invite one person at a time to come up and take a note off the cone—it does not need to be your own—and offer an idea for how we can try to overcome this obstacle. After you have given your idea, anyone else in your small group can offer their ideas before you move to the next person. Continue this until you have talked about all the obstacles on the cone.

3. After all the groups (cones) are free of obstacles, wrap up the activity by making these points:

- We are all called to be disciples of Jesus Christ through our Baptism. To be a disciple means to follow the way of life taught by the Master, even if that way of life isn't always easy.

- We will face obstacles in following Jesus. We will be tempted to sin, tempted to remain quiet when we should speak out about our beliefs, and tempted to disbelieve in God when faced with pain and evil.

- But we can face these obstacles and be stronger for doing so. However, it takes support from each other and trust in God!

Break (11:00 A.M.)

Answering God's Call in Our Work (11:20 A.M.)

In these talks the retreatants are invited to share in the faith stories of two people who live out God's call in their everyday jobs.

Preparation

- Invite two people from different jobs or professions to speak about how they answer God's call in their work. For example, you may want to invite a firefighter and a pipe fitter, a teacher and a gas station owner, or a doctor and a retail clerk. Make sure both people are not from traditional helping professions. Look at the demographics of your parish. If your parish is in a college town, invite a professor. If half of your parishioners are in military families, invite an officer to speak.

  If possible, choose a man and a woman to speak. Consider also the ethnic diversity of your parish when selecting your speakers.

  To help the speakers prepare, give each a copy of resource 10, "Suggestions for Work Talk." You will also want to give the presenter a copy of appendix A, "Helpful Hints for Giving Talks." Be clear that they have only 15 minutes each if there are two speakers or 10 minutes if there are three speakers.

1. Introduce your speakers. Mention that we also answer God's call in the work that we do, even though many people do not think of work in that way. These speakers are here to talk about how they try to answer God's call in their everyday work.

Decide which is better, to have the speakers talk and then allow time for questions, or to allow questions after each speaker finishes. Be sure to thank the speakers for their time and the way they give witness to God's call through their work.

The Rich Young Man (12:00 P.M.)

This activity invites teens to spend quiet time exploring and writing about the call of a person of Scripture, the rich young man.

Preparation

- Gather the following supplies:
    - ❏ journals, one for each retreatant
    - ❏ pens or pencils
    - ❏ a Catholic Bible for each retreatant

- Make a copy of these journaling directions for each participant:

"The Rich Young Man" Journaling Directions

1. Read Matthew 19:16–26 again on your own.

2. Close your eyes and reflect quietly on the passage.

3. Read the Scripture passage again.

4. Answer the following questions in your journal:
    - The rich young man found it hard to part with his possessions. How might money and possessions become obstacles on your path to following Jesus? What other things are holding you back from answering God's call?
    - Jesus challenges the rich young man to sell all his possessions and give the money to the poor. How could you begin to answer this challenge?
    - Jesus says that all things are possible with God. What do you find impossible in your life right now? What do you need to turn over to God?

1. Gather teens together and ask one of them to proclaim Matt. 19:16–26, the story of the rich young man. Hand out the journaling directions, journals, and pens or pencils. Explain the journaling directions and make sure there aren't any questions. Then ask teens to find a quiet place for themselves and tell them that they will have 15 minutes of private time to do their reflecting and journaling.

2. When the time has passed gather the group together. Invite the retreatants to continue writing in their journals throughout the retreat.

Pray Anywhere, Anytime (12:20 P.M.)

Prayer Point: You can pray anywhere at anytime.

Preparation

- Gather the following supplies:
    - ❏ paper cut into 2 inch-by-8-inch strips, one for each retreatant
    - ❏ pens or pencils

1. Ask the young people to spread out and give each other a little space for this activity. Introduce this activity in the following way:

> Now that we are about halfway through our retreat, it is important that we take some time to send an e-mail to God and let him know how everything is going. Since we don't have computer access at this very moment, I'd like you to write your e-mail on a strip of paper. It can be short. It can be about whatever you need to pray about right now. And, please, do this on your own in silence.

2. Give teens about 3 minutes to write. Insist that they remain quiet. Then continue by saying:

> CLICK! (Make sure you say this very loudly and get everyone's attention.)
> Guess what? You just sent an e-mail to God.
> You didn't need a computer.
> You didn't need a keyboard.
> You didn't need a modem.
> You didn't need Internet access.
> And, you didn't even have to worry if too many people were online.

Prayer is the original form of *instant messages*. You can talk with God anywhere. You can talk with God anytime. And, you can be sure that God always gets your message.

Lunch (12:30 P.M.)

Supporting One Another (1:15 P.M.)

Prayer Point: We need to pray for others, and we need to allow others to pray for us.

Preparation

- Gather the following supplies:
  - ❑ large cardboard building blocks (set of 24)
  - ❑ two tables
- Place one table in the center front of your gathering space. Place another table at the farthest corner in the back of your gathering space. Assemble the cardboard blocks and scatter them all over the back table. Do not stack them in any specific, neat order.

1. Ask for a volunteer. Ask that person to go get one block from the back table and bring it to the front. Applaud the effort. Ask the next volunteer to get three blocks from the back table and bring them to the front. Applaud that effort. Ask the third volunteer to get eight blocks from the back table and bring them to the front. Applaud this effort as well.

2. Return all the blocks to the back table. Then ask another volunteer to go to the back table and bring all 24 blocks up to the front in one trip. (Often, she or he is a good sport and gives it a try. Sometimes the person will ask someone for help. Sometimes, you might have to suggest to the person—after awhile—to get some help.)

3. After all the blocks have been transported to the front table and the participants have been applauded for their efforts, ask: "What can you learn about prayer from this activity?"

Summarize their answers by stressing the importance of praying for others. There will be times in their lives—if there haven't been already—when they will find it tough to pray and will need the prayers of others.

God Calls Us Through Others (1:25 P.M.)

Teens are invited to share in the faith stories of two people who were challenged to follow God's call through special people in their lives or through their involvement in an outreach ministry.

Preparation

• Invite one person from your team to talk about a special relative, friend, coach, youth minister, or family member who inspired him or her to answer God's call. Invite another person to talk about how personal involvement in community service or church outreach has inspired him or her to answer God's call in his or her life.

To help the speakers prepare, give each a copy of resource 11, "Suggestions for 'God Calls Us Through Others' Talk." You will also want to give the presenter a copy of appendix A, "Helpful Hints for Giving Talks." Be clear that they each have only 15 minutes for their presentation plus time for questions.

1. Introduce your speakers. Mention that we also hear God's call through other people in our lives. These speakers are here to share how they have heard God calling to them through other people.

Decide which is better, to have both speakers talk and then allow time for questions, or to allow questions after each speaker is finished.

Speak, Lord, Your Servant Is Listening (2:05 P.M.)

This activity invites teens to spend quiet time exploring and writing about the call of a person of Scripture—Samuel.

Preparation

• Gather the following supplies:
  ❑ journals, and pens or pencils
  ❑ a Catholic Bible for each retreatant
• Make a copy of these journaling directions for each participant:

"Speak, Lord, Your Servant Is Listening" Journaling Directions

1. Read 1 Samuel 3:1–10 again on your own.

2. Close your eyes and reflect quietly on the passage.

3. Read the Scripture passage again.

4. Answer the following questions in your journal:
   - At first, Samuel does not realize that God is calling him. He thought it was Eli. What are some of the other voices in your life competing with God for your attention?
   - When Samuel finally realizes it is God calling, he says "Speak, Lord, for your servant is listening." How can you learn to listen more carefully for God calling in your life?
   - God did not give up on Samuel. He kept calling until Samuel recognized him and answered. How does it make you feel to know God will never give up on you?

1. Gather teens together and ask one of them to proclaim 1 Sam. 3:1–10, the story of the call of Samuel. Hand out the journaling directions, journals, and pens or pencils. Explain the journaling directions and make sure there aren't any questions. Then ask teens to find a quiet place to themselves and tell them that they will have 15 minutes of private time to do their reflecting and journaling.

2. When the time has passed gather the group together. Invite teens to continue writing in their journals after the retreat.

Break (2:25 P.M.)

Prayer Brings Balance (2:55 P.M.)

Prayer Point: Prayer can bring balance back into your life and it can keep your life in balance.

Preparation

- Make sure the room you are using has enough space for retreatants to stand up and hold their arms out without touching anyone.

1. Tell the retreatants you have a challenge for them, and they should listen to all the directions and begin only when you say "go!" At your signal, they are to stand on one foot. They may not hold the foot with either hand. They may not prop the foot against the other leg. They may not switch feet during the activity. They may not lean against a chair or table for support. Once that foot touches the floor, they must sit down for the remainder of the activity.

2. Signal "go!" Allow about 5 minutes for this activity. After 5 minutes is up, ask: "What did you learn about prayer from this activity?" Summarize that prayer is a lot like the pole a tightrope walker uses to keep balance while walking along the high wire. Prayer can help us keep our life in balance and can get us back in balance when we feel like we are falling.

God Calls Us Through Music (3:05 P.M.)

One powerful way God calls us is through music and the arts. Teens are invited to rest and listen, and see how God calls them through music.

Preparation

- Gather the following supplies:
  - ❏ various music CDs by Catholic or Christian artists
  - ❏ instrumental or classical music
  - ❏ CD player
- Map out the "play list" for 30 minutes worth of Christian and instrumental music. Include some of your youth group's favorites but, also, introduce them to some new Christian music. If you are not familiar with Catholic musicians, consult other youth ministers in your area or your diocesan office of youth ministry.

1. Introduce the activity like this:

> During our retreat, we discussed a few of the ways God calls us. We also heard witness talks that included calls in different times and different ways. During the next half hour, you have an opportunity to listen to God's call through music.
>
> As you know, music is an important part of our worship as a Christian community. Music is a powerful form of prayer. And you know how important music is in each of your lives. Many of you already know that your music has powerful messages that speak to your life. Consider that God also speaks to us through music, through your music.
>
> We invite you to grab your pillow and find a comfortable spot anywhere in our gathering place. Bring nothing else with you. Give each other some space so you are not distracted by anyone or tempted to have a conversation. You may close your eyes if you want.
>
> We will be playing a variety of music—some familiar, some new to you. Some of the music will have lyrics and some will be instrumental. Relax, and listen to the music, and allow God to speak to you and allow yourself to speak to God.

What Is Your Net Worth? (3:35 P.M.)

This quiet reflection invites teens to contemplate their personal call to discipleship. It also asks them to consider their life's call in light of the Gospel and not just in the context of our culture.

Preparation

- Gather the following supplies:
  - ❏ fish netting (Check your local craft store or home decorating store.)
  - ❏ scissors
  - ❏ light blue, medium blue, and dark blue construction paper
  - ❏ a Catholic Bible for each participant
- Cut fish netting into approximately 6 inch-by-6-inch pieces. Make sure you have a piece for each person attending the retreat.
- Copy each of the following questions on a different color of construction paper.
  - ❏ dark blue—What is your net worth?
  - ❏ medium blue—How does society tell you to determine your net worth?
  - ❏ light blue—What is your net worth as a disciple of Jesus?

  Attach three questions (one of each color) to each piece of net.

1. Gather retreatants in a large group and ask a teen to proclaim Luke 5:1–11. Invite teens to spend some quiet time reflecting on their calls and responses in light of the Scripture reading. This is also an opportunity to reflect on what they have learned during the retreat. It is a challenge to view their calls in light of the Gospel rather than just in the context of our culture.

2. Give each person a piece of net with the three reflection questions and a Bible so they can reread the Scripture passage if they choose. Ask them to follow the questions from dark blue to medium blue to light blue. You may also number the questions. Remind them to keep silent during this part of the retreat so each person can have the quiet and space needed to really reflect on the questions.

Preparation for Liturgy (4:00 P.M.)

In planning the liturgy, keep in mind the themes explored during the retreat. Give each small group a role in preparing for liturgy. Suggestions for the liturgy follow.

Songs

The following songs can all be found in the *Spirit and Song* hymnal, OCP Publications, 1999:

- "The Summons," by John L. Bell
- "Servant Song," by Sr. Donna Marie McGargill
- "Here I Am, Lord," by Dan Schutte
- "Anthem," by Tom Conry
- "I Will Choose Christ," by Tom Booth

- "Go Make a Difference," by Tom Tomaszek and Steve Angrisano
- "The Call," by Tom Franzak

Readings

If you are celebrating liturgy for the weekend, use the readings for that Sunday. If you are celebrating the liturgy during the week, you will want to pick special readings that fit this theme. Look at the following readings from the liturgical year as they seem particularly appropriate.

Second Sunday in Ordinary Time, Cycle B

- first reading: 1 Sam. 3:3–20, 29 (the call of Samuel)
- Psalm response: Ps. 40:2, 4, 7–8, 10 (I come to do your will)
- second reading: 1 Cor. 6:13–15, 17–20 (glorify God in your body)
- Gospel reading: John 1:35–42 (Jesus calls the first disciples)

Prayers of Petition

Team members will write the prayers of petition before the retreat or you can invite the retreatants to write the prayers. Use this as a possible response to the petitions: "Lord, answer when we call."

Environment

You will want to decorate your liturgy environment with pictures of saints and modern-day spiritual heroes who have answered God's call with their lives. You may also encourage the retreatants to create simple banners on poster board or poster paper. A good banner theme would be, "I Have Called You By Name and You Are Mine." Decorate the banners with streamers hanging from them with the names of everyone participating in the retreat.

Closing Liturgy (4:30 P.M.)

Dinner (5:30 P.M.)

Resource 8

Suggestions for "Call and Response" Talk

This talk introduces the theme of the retreat, "call and response," to the retreatants and prepares them for what they are going to experience. You have about 20 minutes for this presentation. The following outline provides ideas and thought starters.

Starting the Talk

You will want to begin this talk by trying out these calls and seeing how your group responds:

You Say	They Should Respond
Knock, knock	Who's there?
Thank you	You're welcome.
The Lord is with you	And also with you.
We are . . .	(high school name)
How are you?	Fine, thank you.

Call and response is a big theme in the Scripture and the Christian spiritual tradition. It is also a reality in our lives whether we realize it or not. It goes both ways, God calls and we respond; we call and God responds.

Reflecting on the Call

- All through the ages God has called people to be in relationship with him—both as individuals and in groups. This is because our God is not a passive God; our God is a God of relationships. This is one of the central meanings of the Trinity.
- In the Scriptures we see God calling Adam and Eve, Noah, and Abraham and Sarah; we see him calling the prophets Samuel and Jeremiah; moving into the New Testament we see God calling Mary; and we witness Jesus' call to the first disciples and all the other people Jesus touched.
- God calls us in many different ways. And God is very persistent. When we don't always answer at first, even if we ignore God for a while, he keeps calling us, keeps on trying to have a relationship with us. And even when we sin and even when we mess up, God keeps calling us back to him.
- You might ask the group, "How is God calling you right now in your life?" Tell how you feel you are being called.

Reflecting on Our Response

- The people God called in the Scriptures responded in many different ways. Just as we have choices about responding to God's call in many different ways.

- Some people in the Scriptures took a leap of faith. Some turned their backs on God. Some had to be swallowed by a whale for God to get their attention.
- Ask the group, "How are you responding to God's call right now in your life?" Share some personal reflections about how you are responding.

God Calls Us Through Other People

- During our retreat, you will be hearing from several speakers who have prepared witness talks. They will share how God touched their lives, how God called them and is still calling them. They will talk about how they respond to God in their lives and how that response has changed over the years.
- We will hear about the call to a vocation: as a priest, sister or brother, lay minister, single person, or married person.
- We will talk about how people in various professions and types of work answer God's call on the job.
- We will talk about the many friends, family members, coaches and teachers who have been the hand of God reaching out to touch us.
- We will also talk about how God calls others through each of you.

God Calls Us Through Scripture and Prayer

- During the retreat we will spend time with the Scriptures, hearing about God's call and the ordinary people who became extraordinary by doing God's will.
- We will spend time sharing and praying the Scriptures so we can be inspired and learn to listen for God speaking to us through the Word.
- We will take time to pray in many ways and learn how to make time for prayer in our busy lives.

A Special Word About Journaling

- Explain how a journal helps us get in touch with our feelings. Why is writing something down often easier than talking about it?
- Because journaling can be a powerful way to get in touch with God's call, during the retreat you will be asked to use a journal to write down reactions to talks and activities.
- Ask the retreatants to bring their journals to every activity during the retreat and to write in them often. Stress the importance of respecting the privacy of each person's journal.
- Encourage the retreatants to take their journals home after the retreat, so they can reflect on them overnight and continue writing in the them.

Blessings and Challenges

- When we talk about God's call and our response, ultimately we are really talking about discipleship and about how we are followers of Jesus Christ.
- So during the retreat, we will also talk about the blessings of discipleship and how we need to follow Jesus in our everyday lives.
- And we will also discover the challenges of discipleship and how following Jesus often clashes with our culture and society.

Closing Remarks

- This whole retreat is a call. Are you open to God calling you on this retreat? Are you ready to respond to that call?
- Be open to all we do in the next two days. Be open to learning more about yourself, others, and God.

Suggestions for Vocational Talk

Thank you for saying yes to sharing a little of your vocational call with the young people on our retreat. The amount of time you have is brief so be sure to consider these suggestions for focusing your presentation.

Share Some of Your Personal Faith Story

- How did you feel called to this specific vocation?
- How do you live out this vocational call in your everyday life?
- What are some of the challenges of responding to God's call in your vocation?
- What are some of the blessings of responding to God's call in your vocation?

Give Retreatants Some Directions for Hearing Their Vocational Calls

- God's call is an ongoing process; we need to pay attention to the patterns and people in our lives.
- God's call is different for each person. How God calls your friends and siblings is not the same as God's call to you.
- Be open to God's call in your life. You are too young to be closed to any possibilities. Look into all the different vocations that are part of the Catholic tradition.

Handout 6

The "Magnificat" Prayer

Left: My soul magnifies the Lord,

and my spirit rejoices in God, my savior,

Right: for he has looked with favor on the lowliness of his servant.

Surely, from now on all generations will call me blessed;

Left: for the Mighty One has done great things for me,

and holy is his name.

Right: His mercy is for those who fear him

from generation to generation.

Left: He has shown strength with his arm;

he has scattered the proud in the thoughts of their hearts.

Right: He has brought down the powerful from their thrones

and lifted up the lowly;

Left: he has filled the hungry with good things,

and sent the rich away empty.

Right: He has helped the servant Israel,

in remembrance of his mercy,

Left: according to the promise he made to our ancestors,

to Abraham and to his descendants forever.

All: Amen

(Luke 1:46–55)

(The adapted prayer is from "Magnificat (Mary's Song)" from *The Catholic Youth Bible,* New Revised Standard Version: Catholic Edition, edited by Brian Singer-Towns [Winona, MN: Saint Mary's Press, 2000], page 1200. Copyright © 2000 by Saint Mary's Press. All rights reserved.)

Suggestions for Work Talk

Thank you for saying yes to sharing with the young people how you answer God's call through your work or your profession. The amount of time you have is brief so be sure to consider these suggestions for focusing your presentation.

Share Some of Your Personal Faith Story

- What is the basic work of your profession?
- How did you discover you were called to this profession?
- How do you live out God's call in your job or profession? Give examples such as: helping others, doing an honest day's work, looking out for coworkers.
- What Gospel values are important in your job?
- What are some of the challenges of living as a Christian in your profession?
- What are some of the blessings of living God's call through your profession?
- How has your job or profession helped your faith to grow?

Give Retreatants Some Directions for Hearing Their Calls

- God's call is an ongoing process; we need to pay attention to the patterns and people in our lives.
- God's call is different for each person. How God calls your friends and siblings is not the same as God's call to you.
- Be open to God's call in your life. You are too young to be closed to any possibilities. Look into all the different vocations that are part of the Catholic tradition.

Resource 11

Suggestions for "God Calls Us Through Others" Talk

Thank you for saying yes to sharing with the young people on our retreat about how you have heard God's call through other people. The amount of time you have is brief so be sure to consider these suggestions for focusing your presentation.

Share Some of Your Own Personal Faith Story

- Share personal stories of people who have touched your faith journey.
- How have you felt God's touch through people's influences on your life?
- How have you lived out God's call through your relationship with others? How have you touched their lives?
- How has your faith in God strengthened your relationships?
- How have you encountered the face of God in parish volunteer work? in community work? in the stranger?
- How do you live out God's call in your everyday life?
- What are some of the challenges of responding to God's call?
- What are some of the blessings of responding to God's call?
- Possibly share a Scripture passage, song, poem, or story that speaks to your call and response.

Give Retreatants Some Directions for Hearing Their Calls

- God's call is an ongoing process; we need to pay attention to the patterns and the people in our lives.
- God's call is different for each person. How God calls your friends and siblings is not the same as God's call to you.
- Be open to God's call in your life. You are too young to be closed to any possibilities. Look into all the different vocations that are part of the Catholic tradition.

Retreat 5

Jesus Calls Us

Introduction

"Jesus Calls Us" challenges teens to look at the way of life that Jesus calls us to live. This retreat provides encouragement that faith is not just a Sunday morning obligation.

This weekend retreat focuses on several calls or challenges:

- the call to be more welcoming to others, to be inclusive rather than exclusive, to accept others the way they are
- the call to have faith like a child, to see the wonder in God's creation, to use our imaginations, to discover that faith can be fun
- the call to be shepherds to others, to use our gifts and talents to bring others closer to God
- the call to change our lives, to take a hard look to see where we need to change, and to forgive and be forgiven
- the call to be peacemakers, to work for peace in our world, in our country, in our community, and in all our relationships
- the call to celebrate our faith, to celebrate the birthday of our church, and recognize the many blessings of being Catholic

Goals

- To challenge the retreatants to spend more time exploring the call of Jesus in the Scriptures
- To help them learn more about themselves and others through community building activities and discussions
- To help them build or strengthen a personal relationship with Jesus Christ
- To challenge them to live out the Gospel message of Jesus Christ and put their faith into action

Schedule

The following sequence for "Jesus Calls Us" is just one suggestion on how to arrange your schedule. Use the column labeled "Actual Plan" to record the activities, sequences, and starting times that will work for you.

Time	Activity Name	Activity Type	Actual Plan
Friday Evening			
7:00 P.M.	Arrival		_____
7:30 P.M.	Welcome and Introduction	Talk	_____
7:50 P.M.	Do You Hear Jesus Calling?	Theme talk	_____
8:10 P.M.	Pull-Ups	Icebreaker	_____
8:30 P.M.	Called to Share	Small-group formation	_____
8:35 P.M.	Tickets	Small-group discussion	_____
9:00 P.M.	Snack Break		_____
9:30 P.M.	Dots	Game	_____
10:00 P.M.	Called to Be Welcoming	Talk	_____
10:20 P.M.	To Be More Welcoming	Small-group presentation	_____
11:00 P.M.	Break		_____
11:15 P.M.	Come Down Out of Your Tree	Night prayer	_____
12:00 A.M.	Lights Out		_____
Saturday			
7:45 A.M.	Rising		_____
8:15 A.M.	When I Was Little, I Used to Pray	Morning prayer	_____
8:30 A.M.	Breakfast		_____
9:00 A.M.	Learning From Children's Games	Icebreaker	_____
9:40 A.M.	Called to Have Childlike Faith	Talk	_____
10:00 A.M.	Lollipops and Questions	Small-group discussion	_____
10:30 A.M.	Children's Images of God	Craft	_____
11:00 A.M.	Serving Snack	Snack	_____
11:20 A.M.	Called to Be Shepherds	Talk	_____
11:40 A.M.	Blindfold Caterpillar	Game	_____

12:05 P.M.	Searching for Sheep	Small-group discussion	_____
12:30 P.M.	Lunch		_____
1:15 P.M.	Making Change	Icebreaker	_____
1:50 P.M.	Called to Change	Talk	_____
2:10 P.M.	Scriptures Call Us to Change	Small-group discussion	_____
2:45 P.M.	Break		_____
3:00 P.M.	The Power to Change Others' Lives	Movie	_____
4:30 P.M.	Letter to Self		_____
5:00 P.M.	Dinner and Break		_____
7:30 P.M.	It's Knot What You Think	Small-group challenge	_____
7:55 P.M.	Called to Be Peacemakers	Talk	_____
8:15 P.M.	Recipe for Peace	Quiet time	_____
8:45 P.M.	Pledge of Nonviolence	Personal commitment	_____
9:15 P.M.	Break		_____
10:00 P.M.	I Would Rather Be Bread	Night prayer	_____

Sunday

7:45 A.M.	Rising		_____
8:15 A.M.	Proclaim the Good News	Morning prayer	_____
8:30 A.M.	Breakfast		_____
9:00 A.M.	Musical Chairs	Icebreaker	_____
9:30 A.M.	The Good News About Being Catholic	Small-group presentation	_____
10:15 A.M.	Birthday Cake Break		_____
10:45 A.M.	Called to Celebrate Our Faith	Talk	_____
11:00 A.M.	Celebrating Our Gifts and Talents	Affirmation	_____
11:45 A.M.	Packing Break		_____
12:30 P.M.	Lunch		_____
1:00 P.M.	Preparation for Closing Liturgy	Eucharist preparation	_____
1:30 P.M.	Closing Liturgy	Celebration of Mass	_____

Detailed Description of Activities for Friday ⎯⎯⎯⎯⎯

Arrival (7:00 P.M.)

Have the retreat team warmly welcome the retreatants as they arrive. Distribute name tags.

Welcome and Introduction (7:30 P.M.)

The welcoming talk is intended to give the retreatants an idea of what to expect, to assure them that the retreat team is there for them, and to introduce journal writing as a way to get the most out of the weekend.

Preparation

- Gather the following supplies:
  - ❏ spiral-bound notebooks or hardbound journals, one for everyone
  - ❏ pens or pencils
- On the front cover of each journal, write the name of a retreatant.
- Ask a young person on the team to prepare a 10-minute opening talk to introduce the theme of the retreat. A young person who has been on retreat before seems better able than others to put retreatant's nervousness and fears to rest. To help the person prepare, give her or him resource 12, "Suggestions for Opening Talk." You will also want to give the presenter a copy of appendix A, "Helpful Hints for Giving Talks."

1. Welcome the young people to the retreat and cover any facility directions and ground rules. Then introduce the team member who will give the opening presentation. Distribute the journals at the end of this talk.

Do You Hear Jesus Calling? (7:50 P.M.)

This talk introduces teens to the theme of the retreat and challenges them to be open to the call of Jesus during this retreat and throughout their lives.

Preparation

- Gather the following supplies:
  - ❏ spiral-bound notebooks or hardbound journals, one for each retreatant
  - ❏ pens or pencils
- Ask a team member to prepare a 15-minute talk to introduce the theme of the retreat. To help the person prepare, give him or her resource 13, "Suggestions for 'Do You Hear Jesus Calling' Talk." You will also want to give the presenter a copy of appendix A, "Helpful Hints for Giving Talks."

1. Introduce the team member giving this talk.

2. After the talk, allow 5 minutes for prayer, reflection, and journal writing.

Pull-Ups (8:10 P.M.)

Pull-ups is a community builder designed to get everyone up and moving, to help break up cliques, and to introduce a sense of fun to the weekend's activities.

Preparation

- Gather the following supplies:
    - ❏ chairs, one for each retreatant
    - ❏ CD player and Christian music CD with upbeat music

1. Begin by arranging the chairs in a circle. Ask everyone to take a seat. Introduce the game in the following way:

> We are going to play a game. It will wake us all up and get us moving around. The game is called pull-ups. In a few minutes I will remove two chairs from the group. The people in those two chairs will stand in the center of the circle. Once the music starts, each will go to someone who is seated, take that person by the hand or arm, and pull him or her out of the chair. They will then take their seats. As soon as a person is pulled up, he or she will go to someone else in the circle and pull that person up and take his or her seat. The object of the game is to NOT be left standing in the middle of the circle when the music stops.
>
> You want to walk fast, but not run. The game isn't called Yank-Up, so you do not want to hurt the person you pull out of the chair. And when someone grabs your hand, you must willingly leave your chair.

You will want to demonstrate with another person as you explain the directions. If people get too rough, just stop the game for a few minutes and remind them of safety.

2. When the game is over, encourage everyone to keep getting to know each other and mixing with new people, even when we aren't playing a game. Welcome the retreatants again and tell them how glad the team is to have them at the weekend retreat.

Called to Share (8:30 P.M.)

This activity divides the retreatants into small community groups for discussions and other activities.

Preparation

- Gather the following supplies:
    - ❏ retreatants' journals
    - ❏ pens or pencils

- Before the retreat, assign the participants to small groups of six to eight people. Try to mix up the shy and rowdy folks. Make sure you have a mix of ages, gender, and ethnicity. Assign one teen team member and one adult team member to each group.
- Assign each group a name that is one of the "Calls of Jesus" used during the retreat: Welcoming, Childlike, Shepherd, Changing, Peacemaker, and Celebrating. In each journal write the name of the group he or she is assigned to on the inside back cover.

1. Ask retreatants to look inside the back covers of their journals. Direct them to find the rest of the people who have the same "Call of Jesus" retreat theme. When they have formed a group, direct each group to find a table and sit together. Tell them this will be their small group for all retreat activities and discussions.

Tickets (8:35 P.M.)

During this discussion retreatants get to know others in their group and start becoming comfortable with small-group sharing.

Preparation

- Gather the following supplies:
  - ❏ a roll of raffle tickets

1. With the retreatants still in their small groups, invite them to take some tickets from your roll. They can take one ticket, two tickets, three tickets, four tickets, or five tickets. They must take at least one and they cannot take more than five. Do not tell them how they will use the tickets.

2. When everyone has raffle tickets, tell the retreatants that they must think of something to share about themselves for each ticket they have. Use the example, "If I have one ticket, I only have to share one thing about myself. If I have five tickets, I must share five things about myself." Each person begins by telling everyone in the group his or her name, and it does not count as one of their tickets. As the leader, you pretend you have five tickets yourself, and share five things about yourself.

3. When all the groups have finished, remind them that a big part of being on retreat is sharing with others who we are. Remark how we found things in common and found many differences—and both are great. We celebrate what we have in common and we celebrate our wonderful differences as well.

Alternatives

- Ask everyone to put their name on the back of each of their tickets. Collect the tickets in a basket and tell the teens there will be a small raffle for attendance prizes throughout the retreat.
- If your group is small, perhaps fifteen to twenty retreatants, you could do this activity with the entire group rather than in small groups.

Snack Break
(9:00 P.M.)

Dots (9:30 P.M.)

Dots is a game that demonstrates how we often exclude others from our groups and the impact that it has on those people.

Preparation

- Gather the following supplies:
  - ❑ small dot stickers in five or more different colors, one dot for each participant

1. Tell the teens that you will be placing a dot on their foreheads. They may not take the dot off and look at it, tell someone else what color dot is on their forehead, or ask about the color of their own dot.

    Place the dots randomly on people's foreheads. Make sure that at least three or four people have the same color dots but give only one teen a single white dot. You will want to choose someone who is outspoken, or one of your team leaders to receive the white dot.

2. When all the dots are given out, ask retreatants to group by the same color dots without speaking. When everyone has found the people with the same color, it will be clear that one person has been left out. Direct the retreatants to gather in their small groups and discuss the following questions:
    - What did you learn from this activity?
    - How did the person with the single dot feel?
    - What does this game teach us about labeling people?
    - What does this game teach us about including others?

Called to Be Welcoming (10:00 P.M.)

Jesus gives us many examples of how we need to be welcoming to others, especially to people who are different or in need. This talk asks teens to examine their lives and find ways to be more welcoming.

Preparation

- Ask a team member to prepare a 15-minute talk on the theme of being welcoming toward other people. To help the person prepare, give him or her resource 14, "Suggestions for 'Called to Be Welcoming' Talk."

1. Introduce the team member giving this talk.

2. After the talk, allow 5 minutes for prayer, reflection, and journal writing.

To Be More Welcoming (10:20 P.M.)

This activity is designed to reinforce the theme of the welcoming talk and spur creativity by asking teens to find ways of welcoming all they meet.

1. In the large group, ask and discuss:
   - What helps you feel welcome when you go somewhere new?
   - What do you do—as an individual—to make others feel welcome?

   Challenge the small groups to think of some creative ways they can greet people and make them feel welcome. They must include everyone in their group in the presentation. Give each group 10 minutes and a private space to work if at all possible. Tell them that when they come back together, they will welcome each other in the large group.

   If they seem confused you might want to give some examples of ways to do this: skits, songs, dances, human sculptures, moving billboards, and so on.

2. After 10 minutes have the groups return and demonstrate their welcoming activities. After the groups' presentations, applaud their efforts and remind them that we need to be welcoming not just for one activity and one retreat, but all year.

Break (11:00 P.M.)

Come Down Out of Your Tree (11:15 P.M.)

Preparation

- Gather the following supplies:
  - ❏ a Catholic Bible marked at Luke 19:1–10
  - ❏ a large candle, matches, and other items used for your prayer environment
- Ask a volunteer to read the Scripture passage. Ask a teen or adult team member to prepare a 5-minute reflection on the reading.

1. Darken your chapel or prayer room and ask everyone to walk quietly into the worship space and sit in a circle on the floor. Then lead the following prayer service.

Call to Prayer

As we close our first evening of retreat, we thank God for the blessings of this day, especially for the chance to welcome and meet new people. Let us pray that this spirit of hospitality continues throughout our weekend together.

Scripture

Light your retreat candle and then have the reader proclaim the story of Jesus and Zacchaeus in Luke 19:1–10.

Reflection

A retreat team member gives a short reflection on the Zacchaeus story. The reflection should emphasize that Jesus made everyone feel welcome—short or tall, fisherman or tax collector, man or woman, children or adults, sick or dying, rich or poor, Jews or Gentiles. Jesus still welcomes everyone today. Give some examples of how people have already been welcoming on the retreat.

Jesus did the calling, but Zacchaeus had to come out of the tree. Come down from your tree; spend some time with Jesus this weekend.

Candlelight Prayer

Introduce this part of the prayer:

> For our prayer tonight, we use three forms of prayer: scripture, symbol (the candle), and shared prayer. We believe that God hears us when we pray everywhere and at any time. We can pray alone anytime, but we also believe in the power of praying together.
>
> As the candle is passed around our group, we invite you to share a short prayer, perhaps a few words or a sentence. You can pray for yourself or others; you can pray to be more welcoming for Jesus, or you can pray for peace. If you don't want to say your prayer out loud, you will simply hold the candle silently for a few seconds before passing it along.
>
> We ask everyone else to be very quiet, out of respect for the person praying and out of respect for the God we pray to.

Closing Blessing

> May God bless you and keep you,
> May the Light of Christ shine upon you,
> May the Holy Spirit bring you peace.
> In the name of the father,
> And of the Son,
> And of the Holy Spirit.
> Amen

Lights Out
(12:00 A.M.)

Detailed Description of Activities for Saturday

Rising (7:45 A.M.)

When I Was Little, I Used to Pray (8:15 A.M.)

Preparation

- Gather the following supplies:
    - ❏ a Catholic Bible marked at Mark 10:13–16
    - ❏ the book, *Old Turtle*, by Douglas Wood and Cheng-Khee Chee (New York: Scholastic Press, 2001)
    - ❏ a large candle, matches, and other prayer environment items
    - ❏ small bottles of bubbles, one for each retreatant
- Ask two teens to prepare a brief 3-minute skit of how they used to pray when they were children. Ideally the skit should be humorous and also make a point about praying with faith.
- Ask for two volunteers, one to be a reader and the other a storyteller.

1. Ask everyone to walk quietly into the worship space and sit in a circle on the floor. When everyone is settled, lead the group in the following prayer service.

Call to Prayer

Light the retreat candle and begin the prayer with these or similar words:

> Dear Jesus, we come to you this morning in anticipation of a new day. Help us to approach this day as an adventure, full of excitement for all you have in store for us. Help us rediscover and reclaim a sense of imagination and wonder.

"When I Was Little" Skit

Invite the two teen team members to present the skit they have prepared. After the skit ask the participants to meditate silently on how they prayed when they were children.

Scripture

The designated reader proclaims Mark 10:13–16, the passage in which Jesus calls us to have faith like a child.

Bubbles Prayer

Give each teen a small bottle of bubbles to play with for about 3 minutes. Then ask: "What did you learn about God by playing with the bubbles this morning?" Thank teens for the variety of answers and challenge them to keep using their imagination to find God throughout the day ahead.

Meditative Reading

Gather teens on the floor around the storyteller. Introduce the book, *Old Turtle* (Wood and Chee, 2001) by acknowledging that as we get older, we forget how great it is to have someone read to us. Yet Jesus, the storyteller, is always ready to teach through stories if we just gather at his feet. Then have the storyteller read the book.

Breakfast (8:30 A.M.)

Learning from Children's Games (9:00 A.M.)

These children's games are a fun way to challenge teens to look for God in the world around them and emphasize the importance of imagination and our faith.

Preparation

- Gather the following supplies:
  - ❑ a paper bag and slips of paper
  - ❑ an assortment of children's toys: yo-yos, marbles, paddle-balls, pinwheels—so that there is at least one toy for every seven participants. Note: You could invite the participants to bring a favorite childhood toy with them to the retreat.
- Write the names of children's games on slips of paper and place them in a paper bag. Here are some possibilities: red light, green light; duck, duck, goose; red rover; follow the leader; Simon says; steal the bacon.

1. Introduce this activity by telling teens that we can find God in all sorts of places and in all sorts of things. When we were little, we loved to play games; we loved to play with toys. We were good at using our imaginations and we gave them plenty of exercise.

   During this activity, the retreatants will be challenged to find God in children's games and children's toys. In other words, we are going to play.

2. Divide teens into groups of seven to eight. Give each small group a slip of paper with a children's game on it. Encourage them to play the game for a little bit and then answer the question: What can we learn about God from this children's game?

3. Give each small group a children's toy. Encourage the groups to play with the toys for a little bit and then answer the question: What can we learn about God from this toy? Ask the groups to select a spokesperson and share their answers with the wider group.

4. Close by encouraging teens to be like children in looking for God everywhere and in everything—and to never lose their imagination.

Called to Have Childlike Faith (9:40 A.M.)

Jesus holds up the faith of a child as a model for our reliance on God. This talk invites teens to recall their approach to God as a child and recapture a sense of wonder.

Preparation

- Ask a team member to prepare a 15-minute talk on the theme of being welcoming toward other people. To help the person prepare, give him or her resource 15, "Suggestions for 'Called to Have Childlike Faith' Talk."

1. Introduce the team member giving this talk.

2. After the talk, allow 5 minutes for prayer, reflection, and journal writing.

Lollipops and Questions (10:00 A.M.)

During this discussion, teens are asked to recall and share their memories of God and faith when they were small children.

Preparation

- Gather the following supplies:
  - ❏ lollipops, ten for each small group
  - ❏ slips of white paper for questions
  - ❏ scotch tape
- Create sets of lollipop questions by copying and attaching each of these ten discussion questions to ten different lollipops. Make a set for each small group.
  - When did you first learn about God?
  - What is the first prayer you ever learned?
  - Who taught you about God when you were little?
  - What was your favorite Bible story when you were little?
  - What can you remember about your first Communion?
  - How can you help children get closer to Jesus?
  - Share a childhood memory about church.
  - How did you view God when you were little?
  - What was your favorite song about God?
  - Are there any children in your life right now who teach you about God?

1. In small groups, ask teens to share their answers to the questions on the lollipops. They can take turns reading the questions, but they all need to share in the discussion.

2. When the discussion is over, they can eat the lollipops!

Children's Images of God (10:30 A.M.)

This craft project asks teens to explore their image of God through finger paints.

Preparation

- Gather the following supplies:
    - ❏ newspapers
    - ❏ finger paints and finger paint paper
    - ❏ disposable aluminum pie tins or cupcake tins
    - ❏ sponges and water
- Cover the painting area with newspapers to make cleanup easier. Pour a little of the finger paint in each pie tin.

1. Introduce this activity in the following way:

    Try to think back to when you were a little child. How did you view God? What was your image of God? We invite you now to go to a finger painting station and return to your childhood days for a few moments. So roll up your sleeves and take off any jewelry on your fingers or hands and use the finger paints to create the image of God you held when you were a little child.

2. When the teens are finished, ask them to leave their paintings to dry and wash their hands before beginning their small group discussion. Then in their small groups have them discuss the following questions:
    - What image of God did you draw?
    - How has your image of God changed since that time?
    - How does your image of God need to change in the future?

3. Close by encouraging teens to constantly grow in the ways they view God, to continue to grow in their relationships with God, and to continue growing in their faith.

Serving Snack (11:00 A.M.)

Preparation

- Gather the following supplies:
    - ❏ items needed to make peanut butter and jelly sandwiches
    - ❏ cookie cutters

1. Tell the young people that today we are having for a snack peanut butter and jelly sandwiches, made with cookie cutters. However, they will not make their own sandwich in order to emphasize that we need to be servants of one another. So they need to find a partner and make a sandwich for that person. Serve their drink. Then, their partner needs to do the same for them.

Called to Be Shepherds (11:20 A.M.)

This talk discusses how Jesus calls each of us to be shepherds. We are called to take care of each other, build community, and bring people closer to God.

Preparation

- Ask a team member to prepare a 15-minute talk on the theme of answering Jesus' call to be shepherds. To help the person prepare, give him or her resource 16, "Suggestions for 'Called to Be Shepherds' Talk."

1. Introduce the team member giving this talk.

2. After the talk, allow 5 minutes for prayer, reflection, and journal writing.

Blindfold Caterpillar (11:40 A.M.)

This game builds trust and communication skills as teens are challenged to consider the role of follower and leader.

Preparation

- Gather the following supplies:
  - ❏ blindfolds, one for each group member
- Prior to the meeting, scout out an area outdoors, or a big open space for this activity. Choose a route for the "caterpillar" that is safe from dangerous obstacles.

1. Divide the participants into groups of eight to ten people. Designate one person in the group as the guide. Brief the guides (away from the others) on the route the "caterpillars" are to travel. Give the others the blindfolds and ask them to put them on.

2. Line up the blindfolded participants of each group single file, so if you have three groups, you will have three short single-file lines. Direct the people in the lines to place their hands on the shoulders of the people in front of them. Tell the guides to begin directing their "caterpillar" on how to travel the designated route. The guides may only speak; they may not guide the caterpillar, for example, by taking the hand of the person at the front of the line.

    If time permits, the person giving the directions can switch with someone else in the line.

3. After you have given the groups a few minutes to navigate the course, gather everyone together and discuss the following questions:
    - What did it feel like to be the leader? What did you learn about being a leader from this activity?
    - What did it feel like to be a follower? What did you learn about being a follower from this activity?
    - What can you learn about Jesus, the Good Shepherd from this activity?

4. Close by reminding teens that it is important that they know who they are following throughout their lives and that it is never a good idea to follow blindly.

Searching for Sheep (12:05 P.M.)

This activity invites teens to search for the qualities of a good leader. The questions also challenge teens to answer Jesus' call to be a shepherd to others.

Preparation

- Gather the following supplies:
  - ❏ large paper, markers, and scissors
  - ❏ paper and pens or pencils
- Create twelve sheep posters using the large paper and scissors. You will want to start with one as a template and use it to create the others. Write one of the following questions on each sheep poster. Prior to the session hide the posters in various places around the retreat grounds.

  1. What are some words to describe a good leader?
  2. How does a good leader treat the people who follow her or him?
  3. How does a good leader keep people from being left out?
  4. How does a good leader make others feel welcome?
  5. How should we decide who we will follow?
  6. Why do we need both followers and leaders?
  7. Who are some of the leaders you look up to?
  8. How have you been a leader for others?
  9. What are some of the qualities of Jesus, our good shepherd, and leader?
  10. How can we each take a leadership role in the church?
  11. Jesus says, "I know my own [sheep] and my own [sheep] know me" (John 10:14). How can we get to know Jesus better?
  12. Jesus says, "I know my own [sheep] and my own [sheep] know me" (John 10:14). How can we do a better job of reaching out to others in need?

1. Give each small group paper and pencils. Direct the groups to find the twelve sheep posters you have hidden. When they find a poster, ask them to write the question on their paper and talk about it briefly before they look for the next question. When they have found and answered all twelve questions, they are to return to the main meeting area.

2. When all the groups have returned, ask each group to choose one question and spend a few minutes discussing it further. Ask a spokesperson from each small group to share its answer with the entire group. (This activity is adapted from *Growing With Jesus*, 1993, pp. 36–37.)

Lunch (12:30 P.M.)

Making Change (1:15 P.M.)

This icebreaker uses pocket change to introduce the idea that we all need change in our lives and identify the areas on which we need to work.

Preparation

- Gather the following supplies:
  - ❑ a variety of coins: pennies, nickels, dimes, and quarters
  - ❑ a copy of handout 7, "Making Change: Jesus Calls Us to Change Our Lives," for each participant
- In the list of what to bring on the retreat, ask the young people to bring some change (coins).

1. Tell everyone that for the next activity, you are going to ask them to make change—not just for a dollar, but to think about ways they can change their lives for the better. Ask them to dig out the change (coins) they brought with them on the retreat. Give them each a copy of handout 7, "Making Change: Jesus Calls Us to Change Our Lives." Note: Make sure you have some extra change available in case someone forgets to bring coins with them.

2. Now direct them to move around the meeting space and pair up with someone they don't know well. They are to give each other a coin. Then they must answer a question from the handout under the category of coin they received. For example, if someone receives a quarter, that person must pick and answer a question under the quarter section on the handout.

    Ask teens to only share their answers in pairs and to switch partners after each set of questions. The goal is to get around the room and talk to as many people as possible.

Called to Change (1:50 P.M.)

This talk gets across that change isn't easy, but following Jesus requires that we change our lives to walk in his ways.

Preparation

- Ask a team member to prepare a 15-minute talk on the theme of answering Jesus' call to change our lives. To help the person prepare, give him or her resource 17, "Suggestions for 'Called to Change' Talk."

1. Introduce the team member giving this talk.

2. After the talk, allow 5 minutes for prayer, reflection, and journal writing.

Scriptures Call Us to Change (2:10 P.M.)

During this discussion, teens break open the word of God and identify the challenges or the call to change in each passage.

Preparation

- Gather the following supplies:
  - ❏ a Catholic Bible for each small group
- Prepare a small slip of paper for each small group with one of the following Bible passages written on the slip. Note: These are the readings for cycle A of Lent. You will want to use the readings for the cycle and liturgical season in which you are holding the retreat.
  - Matt. 4:1–11—Jesus is tempted in the desert
  - Matt. 17:1–9—The transfiguration
  - John 4:5–15—The woman at the well
  - John 9:1–12—Jesus and the blind man
  - John 11:17–44—The raising of Lazarus

1. Introduce this activity by sharing with teens that the Bible is not just a book that should sit on the table and collect dust. The Scriptures have the potential to transform our lives if we just break open the word of God and accept its challenge.

   Then give each group a Bible and one of the slips with the Gospel passages. Ask the retreatants to read over the passages in their small groups and do two things. Discuss the question, "How is Jesus calling us to change in this passage?" Then write a prayer asking God to help us answer this call to change during Lent.

2. Bring the groups back together and ask a spokesperson from each group to share its answer and its prayer with the entire group. Close by encouraging teens to spend time reading the Scriptures.

Break (2:45 P.M.)

The Power to Change Others' Lives (3:00 P.M.)

The inspiring movie *Pay It Forward* (Warner Bros., 2000, 123 minutes) shows how one person can make a tremendous difference in the lives of others.

Preparation

- Gather the following supplies:
  - ❏ a large screen television and VCR/DVD
  - ❏ a copy of the movie *Pay It Forward*

1. Invite the participants to get their pillows and get comfortable because they are going to watch a movie. Tell them that they are going to see a movie with a message about the power we have to change the world. Then begin the movie. Note: Most home video and DVD copyright agreements require you to receive special permission or have an umbrella license before showing movies to a group. If you are not sure if you have such a license check with your pastor or diocesan legal office.

Alternatives

If you are at a facility with outdoor recreational opportunities you will want to use this time for that purpose and show the movie after dinner. Or, this time can be used to have a sacrament of Reconciliation (also called Penance) service and private confessions if a priest is available.

Letter to Self (4:30 P.M.)

This quiet activity introduces solitude as an important way to explore where we are in our lives right now and where we strive to be.

Preparation

- Gather the following supplies:
    - ❏ envelopes and writing paper
    - ❏ pens or pencils

1. After the movie, give each teen an envelope, writing paper, and a pen or pencil. Introduce this activity by sharing with teens that sometimes our lives get so busy and noisy that we fail to take quiet time for ourselves and to spend time talking with God. Then ask them to write their own name and complete address on the envelope.

2. Now invite them to write a letter to God about how they would like to change their lives during Lent (or Advent). Refer them to the activities and discussions you have already had in this session: the coin activity, the scripture sharing, the movie, and the other retreat experiences up to this time. Those should be a starting point for a heart-to-heart talk with God.

    To write their letters ask them to find a place apart from others where they can think, pray, and write. Ask them to respect the silence for themselves and others during this activity. Note: This activity is a great one to do outside if weather permits.

Dinner and Break (5:00 P.M.)

It's Knot What You Think (7:30 P.M.)

During this activity teens must work together to untangle a knot of hands, building teamwork and cooperation.

1. Divide teens into groups of eight and then give the following instructions:

> In your small group, stand in a circle shoulder to shoulder. Put your arms straight out in the center of the circle. Grab the hand of two different people in your group. You may not grab the hand of the people on either side of you. (Make sure there are no loose arms before continuing.)
>
> The object is to untangle the human knot without letting go of the arms you have grabbed. You may move around, over, or under, but do not break any connections.

When you are sure everyone understands the directions give the signal to begin.

2. Some groups will finish before others, but make sure to allow time for all the groups to finish. If a group is having a difficult time, invite another group that has finished to help out.

When all the groups have untangled themselves gather everyone back into the large group and ask the following questions:

- What made it tough to untangle the knot? What made it easier?
- What did you need in order to untangle the knot?
- What can we learn from this game about working with others?
- What can we learn about peacemaking from this game?

Close by encouraging everyone to find new ways to cooperate and build teamwork together. Challenge them to find creative and fun ways to be peacemakers. (This activity is adapted from *Vine & Branches,* vol. 1, p. 103.)

Called to Be Peacemakers (7:55 P.M.)

This talk is on how Jesus calls us to be more peaceful in our words and actions, and to be peacemakers in our relationships with others.

Preparation

- Ask a team member to prepare a 15-minute talk on the theme of answering Jesus' call to be peacemakers. To help the person prepare, give her or him resource 18, "Suggestions for 'Called to Be Peacemakers' Talk."

1. Introduce the team member giving this talk. After the talk, allow 5 minutes for prayer, reflection, and journal writing.

Recipe for Peace (8:15 P.M.)

During this activity, teens are asked to reflect on their definition of peace, what Jesus teaches us about peace, and how we can be more peaceful.

Preparation

- Gather the following supplies:
  - ❏ blank recipe/index cards, one for each retreatant
  - ❏ pens or pencils

1. Give out the pens and recipe cards. Ask teens not to start writing until you are finished with the directions. Introduce the activity like this:

> Think about the word *peace*. What does it mean? What do you need to make peace?
>
> For the next few minutes, we are going to ask you to spread out and take some quiet time for yourself. During this time, you will write your own personal recipe for peace. There are no right or wrong answers. Think about what Jesus has taught us about peace; think about what you have learned during our retreat; think about how recent world events have touched your life; think about areas in your own life where you need to be more peaceful.

When you are finished with the directions invite the teens to find their quiet spot and begin writing. Remind them to stay quiet if some forget.

2. After all are finished, encourage them to take their recipe home and put it up somewhere in their room where they can see it every day and be reminded to keep working for peace.

Pledge of Nonviolence (8:45 P.M.)

During this discussion, teens brainstorm strategies for being peacemakers and take a pledge to work for peace.

Preparation

- Gather the following supplies:
    - ❑ a copy of handout 8, "Pledge of Nonviolence," for each retreatant
    - ❑ ruled yellow paper and pens or pencils
- Make one large copy of the pledge for all to sign.

1. Give out copies of the "Pledge of Nonviolence" and give everyone time to read it. Then ask the young people to return to their small groups and choose a recorder and a spokesperson.

    Next, assign each group to pick one line of the pledge to work on. Ask the groups to each think of five concrete things or strategies that they can do to put their part of the pledge into action.

2. When the groups are finished, ask a spokesperson from each group to share its ideas on putting the pledge into action. Close by asking each person to sign the master copy of the pledge. They can take their copies home.

Break (9:15 P.M.)

I Would Rather Be Bread (10:00 P.M.)

Preparation

- Gather the following supplies:
  - ❏ two copies of resource 19, "I Would Rather Be Bread" (Maryann Hakowski, *Vine & Branches,* p. 47)
  - ❏ a Catholic Bible, marked at John 8:2–11
  - ❏ stones, one for each participant
  - ❏ a loaf of bread in a clear, plastic bag
- Have a team member prepare a very short reflection on the Scripture reading of the woman caught in adultery, John 8:2–11. The focus should be that peace begins when we realize we have no right to throw stones.
- Recruit two readers to read the dialogue, "I Would Rather Be Bread." Ask them to practice before the prayer.
- Choose a song to begin and close the prayer. Consider using a song like "Peace Prayer" by John Foley, S.J. (Phoenix, AZ: North American Liturgy Resources, 1975, no. 40) to begin and a song like "Bread for the World" by Bernadette Farrell, *Breaking Bread* (Portland, OR: OCP Publications, 2002, no. 349) to close.
- Before the prayer service begins, place a loaf of bread near the retreat candle in the center of your space. Surround and cover the bread with stones.

1. Begin by asking everyone to enter the chapel or prayer space quietly and to take a seat. Light the retreat candle and lead the prayer service using the following outline.

Call to Prayer

> Are you holding rocks in your hands? Are you holding onto rocks and don't even know it? Just imagine all that you could hold in your hands, in your heart, if you let go of your rocks. Come, sit a while. Come, pray a while. Come and let go of your rocks.

Opening Song

Dialogue: "I Would Rather Be Bread"

After everyone is absolutely quiet, the two readers come forward and begin their dialogue. After the dialogue is finished, the pair bow quietly and take their seats.

Scripture Reading: John 8:2–7

Reflection

Have someone offer a short reflection on the Scripture reading, connecting it to the dialogue.

Shared Prayer

Invite the retreatants to offer a prayer for peace somewhere in the world and after they do to remove one of the stones from the pile and place it outside the circle. Note: You may want to have the teens sign their personal copies of the "Pledge of Nonviolence" here as part of the prayer service.

Closing Song

Detailed Description of Activities for Sunday

Rising (7:45 A.M.)

Proclaim the Good News (8:15 A.M.)

Preparation

- Gather the following supplies:
  - ❏ a candle, matches, and other prayer environment items
  - ❏ other supplies as determined
- Prior to the retreat, ask five team members to prepare a proclamation of the Good News as described below. This service will vary from group to group based on your gifts and talents.

1. Ask everyone to walk quietly into the worship space and sit in a circle on the floor.

2. Light the retreat candle and lead the prayer using the following outline.

Call to Prayer

A proclamation of the Good News of Jesus Christ according to the teens of (insert parish or school name here).

Proclamation of the Good News

For this, retreat team members need to develop several different ways of proclaiming the Good News based on their gifts and talents. Some ways are suggested below. You also need to decide on a group response after each proclamation. It can be a simple spoken response as indicated below or you could choose the refrain from a song to sing.

First Proclamation: Scripture reading (look at Mic. 6:6–8 or 1 Sam. 3:1–10)
All: Go out to all the world and proclaim the Good News
Second Proclamation: contemporary Christian music
All: Go out to all the world and proclaim the Good News
Third Proclamation: short witness talk
All: Go out to all the world and proclaim the Good News
Fourth Proclamation: teach sign language for "Here I am Lord"
All: Go out to all the world and proclaim the Good News

Fifth Proclamation: a dance to symbolize God's call and our responses
All: Go out to all the world and proclaim the Good News

Breakfast (8:30 A.M.)

Musical Chairs (9:00 A.M.)

This variation of the popular party game is a springboard to sharing about the celebrations in our lives, and helps us recognize that we need to celebrate our faith.

Preparation

- Gather the following supplies:
  - ❏ chairs
  - ❏ CDs, boom box
- Set up chairs in two rows facing each other. There should be enough chairs so there is one per person minus one.
- Prepare some questions related to our theme of celebrating our faith to start the musical chairs. Write at least ten (you can choose from these and/or create your own).
  - What is your favorite holiday celebration? Why?
  - Who are some of the people in your life you would like to celebrate?
  - What is your favorite church holiday? Why?
  - What can we celebrate about being teens?
  - If you could design your own party hat, what would it say?
  - What color balloon would you pick to describe yourself? Why?
  - How did Jesus celebrate with his friends?
  - What wish will you make next time you blow out the candles on your birthday cake?
  - What are some things to celebrate about your parish?
  - What is the best family celebration you have ever attended? Why?
  - How do we celebrate our faith when we attend Mass together?

1. Refresh everyone's memory on how to play musical chairs. While the music is playing, everyone walks around the chairs in a clockwise direction. When the music stops, they sit down in the closest chair.

   However, this icebreaker is a little bit different from usual musical chairs. When the music stops, the person left out picks a question to ask the entire group. Participants answer the question only with the person across from them—in pairs. When the music starts again, the question reader rejoins the circle and tries not to be the person left out the next time the music stops. When you are sure everyone understands the directions begin the game.

2. After the group has answered the questions you have prepared, invite them to write some questions of their own. Remind them that our theme is Jesus calls us to celebrate our faith. Play for another 10 minutes or so.

Close by reminding teens that we have a lot to celebrate—as teens, as members of our parish, and as part of the Catholic Church. Encourage them to keep celebrating their faith throughout the year.

The Good News About Being Catholic (9:30 A.M.)

This activity challenges teens to find creative ways to celebrate their faith and share the Good News.

Preparation

- Gather the following supplies:
  - ❏ poster paper, markers, and other art supplies
  - ❏ a box of costumes and props

1. Introduce the activity like this:

These days the news seems to be filled with scandal including negative news about the Catholic Church. Our Church has experienced some very tough problems, and these tend to give Catholics a bad name.

We as Catholics, as people of faith, as members of our parish (or school) have a lot to celebrate. It is time to get the Good News out there.

In your small groups, come up with one way the Catholic Church spreads the Good News—preferably something that you yourselves have experienced. You can do the following:
- Create a TV spot.
- Design a highway billboard.
- Do a TV news interview.
- Write new lyrics to a popular song.
- Create a top ten list.

2. Give the groups about 15 minutes to work and then invite them to share their advertisements for the Good News with the larger group. Close by telling them not to be discouraged about bad news about the Church, but to continue to look for all the great and wonderful things happening, especially here in our own community.

Birthday Cake Break (10:15 A.M.)

Celebrate Pentecost by having a birthday cake for a snack. We can think of Pentecost as the birthday of the church—don't forget to make a wish and blow out the candles.

Called to Celebrate Our Faith (10:45 A.M.)

Our faith is a celebration and we are all invited to the party. This talk makes that point and invites the young people to take pride in being Catholic and to make time for God!

Preparation

- Ask a team member to prepare a 15-minute talk on the theme of answering Jesus' call to change our lives. To help the person prepare, give him or her resource 20, "Suggestions for 'Called to Celebrate Our Faith' Talk."

1. Introduce the team member giving this talk. After the talk, allow 5 minutes for prayer, reflection, and journal writing.

Celebrating Our Gifts and Talents (11:00 A.M.)

This affirmation activity gives teens the opportunity to celebrate each other through words of encouragement.

Preparation

- Gather the following supplies:
  - ❏ posterboard, a half sheet for each retreatant
  - ❏ markers and tape
- Make a poster following the directions below so you have an example to show as you introduce this activity.

1. Give each teen a half sheet of posterboard. It should be cut in the shape of a large megaphone. On the top of the megaphone poster each teen should write her or his own name and the following phrase: "(My Name) hears the call of Jesus."

2. Hang these "Call" posters up around the room, but low enough so all can reach them. Stress the importance of pointing out the gifts we see in each person and affirming one another. Ask teens to think about one gift, talent, or ability for each person on the retreat and write it on the person's poster. Insist upon only positive qualities being written on the posters, and stay away from superficial comments like "nice hair."

   Tell the retreatants to first write on the posters of members of their own small group because *(1)* the small-group members have had more time to get to know one another, and *(2)* it assures that every person will have at least five or six affirmations on his or her poster.

3. Tell the teens they are welcome to take the posters home after the retreat as a reminder that they all have gifts worth celebrating. Encourage them to build each other up, to support each other, and to celebrate each other beyond the retreat weekend.

Packing Break (11:45 A.M.)

Take some time before lunch to have the retreatants pack their things.

Lunch (12:30 P.M.)

Preparation for Closing Liturgy (1:00 P.M.)

Use this time to prepare for your closing liturgy. The goal is to have all the retreat participants participate in the preparation for the Eucharist.

Preparation

- Gather the following supplies:
  - ❑ all the items necessary for a Eucharist celebration
  - ❑ a sheet of newsprint
- Prepare your celebrant to weave the different calls of Jesus discussed on the retreat into his homily.
- Prepare a sign-up list on a sheet of newsprint listing the groups needed to prepare for the liturgy. Assign a team member to work with each group. Hang this in the morning and have everyone sign up to help during break or lunch. Things you will want to include on the sign-up are:
  - choir and musicians to choose and lead the songs
  - lectors to prepare to proclaim the Scriptures
  - a group to prepare and read the Prayers of the Faithful
  - a group to bring up the gifts of bread and wine as well as other items that symbolize the themes of the retreat
  - a group to prepare the environment by arranging the prayer space and creating special banners

1. After lunch give each group that has signed up its task.

2. Assign the groups places to work. Make sure they know they only have a half hour to work.

Closing Liturgy (1:30 P.M.)

Conclude your retreat experience with a joyful liturgy. You will have to recruit a priest far in advance and work with him in planning any special elements for the liturgy. Before the closing song, it would be appropriate to thank the team, give any final directions, and encourage the retreatants to continue living what they have learned and experienced over the weekend.

Suggestions for Opening Talk

This talk introduces the retreat team and prepares the retreatants for what they are going to experience during the weekend. You have about 10 minutes for this presentation. The following provides ideas and thought starters.

Welcome

Greet the retreatants and let them know how happy the team is that they decided to come. Then introduce the team members. Share your own retreat experiences by talking about some of the following:

- Your reasons for being part of the retreat team.
- Your fears about your first retreat—how you reacted to the other people, the talks, and the activities.
- How your feelings changed throughout your first retreat experience and how your retreat changed your relationship with God.

Emphasize that everyone has something valuable to share and that everyone will have an important part in making the retreat weekend a success. Encourage the retreatants to be open to the touch of others and the touch of God.

Introduction to Journal Writing

Explain that some of the weekend will be spent writing in a journal. A journal helps us get in touch with our feelings. Why is writing something often easier than talking about it?

Discuss the way the retreatants will use their journals to write reactions to talks and activities. Ask everyone to bring their journals to every activity during the weekend—and to write in it often. Stress the importance of respecting the privacy of each person's journal.

Encourage the retreatants to take their journals home after the retreat, so they can reflect on their weekend and continue writing in them.

Resource 13
Suggestions for "Do You Hear Jesus Calling?" Talk

This talk introduces the overall theme of the retreat, "Jesus Calls Us." You have about 15 minutes for this presentation. The following outline provides ideas and thought starters.

Do You Hear God Calling?

Start by reading the story of Jesus calling the first disciples from one of the Gospels: Matt. 4:18–22; Mark 1:16–20; or Luke 5:1–11. Share your own thoughts on the story. The following questions will help you get started.

- Do you hear Jesus calling you as he did these first disciples?
- What does Jesus want me to do with my life?
- How are you called to make a difference in this world?

Share a personal story of a time when you were seeking answers about what to do with your life and how you found guidance from the call of Jesus.

Remind the retreatants that Jesus calls each one of us just as he called those first disciples. We just have to know where to look and what to listen to. In this retreat we encourage you to listen for Jesus' call in prayer, in the Scriptures, and through other people.

God is Persistent

God is constantly reaching out to us. Sometimes we put God on hold. But don't let that happen this weekend—be open to how God is calling you this weekend. Here are some of the things we should listen for on this retreat.

Jesus Calls Us to Welcome Others

- How did Jesus treat everyone with respect?
- How can we be more welcoming in our words and actions?

Jesus Calls Us to Have Faith Like a Child

- How did you view God when you were little?
- How can we regain a sense of wonder and awe in God's creation?

Jesus Calls Us to Be Shepherds for Others

- What are the qualities of a Christian leader?
- How can we lead others to the Father?

Jesus Calls Us to Change Our Lives

- What do I need to change about myself and the way I treat others?
- How is the Gospel a radical call to change?

Jesus Calls Us to Be Peacemakers

- How can I be a person of peace in my words and actions?
- How is Jesus our model for a peacemaker?

Jesus Calls Us to Celebrate Our Faith

- How can we proclaim the Good News?
- What is the Good News about being Catholic?

Closing

Close by being enthusiastic about what you will be doing together on our retreat: Listening to the call of Jesus and answering his call. Encourage the retreatants to be open to the call that Jesus has placed in their heart this weekend.

Resource 14

Suggestions for "Called to Be Welcoming" Talk

This talk explores Jesus' call to be welcoming of all people and how we can be more welcoming to people. You have about 15 minutes for this presentation. The following provides ideas and thought starters.

Scripture Passages

In your talk bring in at least one Scripture passage to illustrate how Jesus calls us to be welcoming. The main passage you should consider is Luke 19:1–10 in which Jesus calls the unpopular tax collector Zacchaeus. Other passages you could consider are:

- John 4:1–15—The woman at the well
- Luke 17:11–19—The ten lepers
- Mark 2:1–12—The man lowered through the roof

Belonging

- Share a time when you felt left out, when someone excluded you from a group. How did it make you feel?
- Share a time when you were part of a group that left someone out. Why did you lack the courage to step out and include the other person?

Make the point that we all need to belong, to be part of a group, to be connected to other people. Healthy groups support members and welcome others.

Jesus Welcomes Everyone

- How do differences sometimes make it tough to accept others?
- How can we focus on what we have in common instead of our differences? Who takes the first step?

Make the point that no one was a stranger to Jesus. He treated each person with dignity and respect. Jesus didn't turn people away if they were a sick man lowered through the roof, a Roman soldier whose daughter was sick, a leper who came seeking a cure, or a Samaritan woman shunned by the Jews. What are some other examples of how Jesus made others feel welcome?

- Jesus was particularly fond of people who were left out.
- Who are the people in our lives who are on the fringes?

Putting Faith Into Action

- How does our church community or youth group welcome others? How can we do it better?
- If we take the time to get to know someone, we are likely to find something we have in common.

Give some concrete examples of how we can make people welcome:

- Get to know people by name.
- Talk to them and listen.
- Invite them to sit with you and to be part of your activity.
- Talk less about yourself and more about them.

Closing

If you are a person who feels left out sometimes, know you are welcome here. We are always welcome to be with Jesus. We are never alone. Jesus always welcomes us. Come on in and stay awhile.

Resource 15

Suggestions for "Called to Have Childlike Faith" Talk

This talk explores Jesus' call to have faith like a child. You have about 15 minutes for this presentation. The following provides ideas and thought starters.

Scripture Passages

In your talk bring in at least one Scripture passage to illustrate how Jesus calls us to be welcoming. The main passage to use is Mark 10:13–16 in which Jesus holds up a child as a model of faith. Other passages you could consider are:

- Matt. 19:13–15—Let the children come to me
- Luke 10:38–42—Martha sits at Jesus' feet

When We Were Little

Begin by sharing some of your childhood memories related to your faith. For example your parents reading the Bible to you, going to church with your parents, attending vacation Bible school, or saying bedtime prayers. Reflect on:

- When you were little, how did you view God?
- What are some of the first prayers you learned?

You will want to bring a picture from your First Communion, sing a children's song, or read a children's story about God.

Now That I Am Older

Take some time to reflect on where God is in your life right now.

- How do you pray? How do you view God?
- Why do we stop praying when we get older? Do we give it up like Santa Claus and the Easter Bunny?
- Have we started to see church as an obligation rather than fun?

To Have Faith Like a Child

What did Jesus mean in calling us to have faith like a child?

- It means having a sense of wonder in all God has created in each of us and the world.
- It means being humble enough to sit at the feet of Jesus and learn something.
- It means trusting God to be there for us and get us through anything.
- It means loving God with our whole heart and allowing the love of God into our lives.

We need to grow in faith throughout our lives by learning more about God and our faith. We do this by reading the Scriptures, by spending time in prayer, and by going to Mass and receiving the Sacraments.

Closing

We can't stay little forever. We need to grow in faith and in our relationship with God. But we must not lose that childlike sense of wonder and recognition that we need God in our lives. Find the fun and playfulness in your prayer and your faith.

Resource 16

Suggestions for "Called to Be Shepherds" Talk

This talk explores Jesus' call to be shepherds, caring for other people. You have about 15 minutes for this presentation. The following provides ideas and thought starters.

Scripture Passages

In your talk bring in at least one Scripture passage to illustrate how Jesus calls us to be welcoming. The main passage to use is John 10:1–18 in which Jesus calls himself the Good Shepherd. Other passages you could consider are:

- Luke 15:1–7—Parable of the lost sheep
- John 21:15–19—Feed my lambs

The Call to Lead

- What if everyone in your church was a follower?
- What if people never came out of their pews?

We need to be more than just followers in the flock of Jesus. He calls us to be shepherds of the Gospel through word and action.

Share some examples of how Jesus, the Good Shepherd, cared for his flock and led people to his Father. How did Jesus care for people? How did he build community? How did he bring people closer to God?

Qualities of a Shepherd

Share a personal story about someone who has been a good shepherd, someone who has been a caring leader and role model for you. Share some qualities that make for a good shepherd or leader.

Share that there are many ways that we can be shepherds in our church, in school, and in our jobs. How can we care for people? How can we build community? How can we bring people closer to God?

Share some of the ministries in which your parish is involved. Give examples of ministries that are open to teens.

When the Going Gets Tough

Being a shepherd isn't always easy or safe. Sometimes the flock or the shepherd is attacked. But a good shepherd doesn't leave the sheep when the going gets tough. What are some things that challenge our ability to be faithful in serving others?

Perhaps one of the hardest challenges is sharing your faith with others. Why is that an important part of being a shepherd? What are some of the ways you can bring other teens closer to Jesus?

Closing

Living like Jesus is much more than a game of "Follow the Leader." No one is perfect—sometimes we'll fail. But the important thing is that we strive to live like Jesus. Real shepherds build community, and never lose sight of the one lost sheep. When we do this, we are answering Jesus' call.

Making Change: Jesus Calls Us to Change Our Lives

When you receive a coin, pick a matching question and answer it as best you can.

Penny Questions

- What is one good change you have been through?
- What is one tough change you have been through?
- What are some changes you are dealing with right now?

Nickel Questions

- What do I need to change in my school life?
- What do I need to change in the way I treat myself?
- What do I need to change in the way I treat others?

Dime Questions

- Why should we change?
- What is the difference between changing for yourself and changing because others want us to change?
- When I change, how does it affect others?
- Why do we sometimes need help to change?

Quarter Questions

- Why is it so hard to change sometimes?
- What do I need to change in my relationship with God?
- How can I change to be more like Jesus?
- How can I change the world—a little bit at a time?

Dollar Question

- Your choice, answer any question above or make up your own question and answer it.

Resource 17

Suggestions for "Called to Change" Talk

This talk explores Jesus' call to change our lives. You have about 15 minutes for this presentation. The following provides ideas and thought starters.

Scripture Passages

In your talk bring in at least one Scripture passage to illustrate how Jesus calls us to change. The main passage to use is Matt. 19:16–30, the story of the rich, young man and Jesus. Other passages you could consider are:

- Luke 15:11–32—The prodigal son
- Luke 6:27–36—Love your enemies
- Luke 13:6–9—The barren fig tree

Call to Change

The Gospels are a call to change. Think about the Gospel readings from the last few Sundays. What is the call to change in those readings? Share some thoughts with the retreatants.

Share a story from your own life about how you've been called to change by the Scriptures. Or you may want to use a contemporary song or refer to a movie that deals with change and conversion. Some Christmas movies deal with this theme, such as *It's a Wonderful Life* and *A Christmas Carol.*

Change is Tough

Change is tough. We get set in our ways. We want to do things the way we always have done them. We promise we won't gossip, but it is easy to slip. We promise to be patient, and then lose our tempers.

- When I change, how does it affect others?
- Why does change need to come from within?
- What do I need to change in the way I treat myself? others? God?

We need to pray every day, asking God to help us have the courage to change.

Seasons of Change

The Church's calendar provides us with two times when it is especially appropriate to consider the need for change, Advent and Lent. We should take time during these seasons to prayerfully look at the need for change in our lives.

The sacrament of Reconciliation also offers us the chance to admit what we have done wrong, seek forgiveness from God, and start anew to make a change in our lives.

Closing

Following Jesus isn't easy. The Gospel message is pretty radical. We need to spend time with the Scriptures, take the message to heart, and start working to change how we live day to day.

Suggestions for "Called to Be Peacemakers" Talk

This talk explores Jesus' call to be peacemakers. You have about 15 minutes for this presentation. The following provides ideas and thought starters.

Scripture Passages

In your talk bring in at least one Scripture passage to illustrate how Jesus calls us to be peacemakers. The main passage to use is John 20:19–23, the story in which the resurrected Jesus gives his peace to the Apostles. Other passages you could consider are:

- Matt. 5:1–12—Blessed are the peacemakers
- Matt. 5:43–48—Love your enemies

What Is Peace?

Consider the following questions. You may even want to start by asking the group how it would answer them.

- What is this fragile thing called peace?
- What does it mean to be peaceful, full of peace?
- What does it mean to be a peacemaker?

Then share with the group that Jesus makes it clear that peace begins with "me." Each of us needs to be a person of peace in our words and actions. What does this imply about the television we watch, the video games we play, the movies we go see, the CDs we listen to? Consider sharing a personal story about one of the following questions:

- How have you brought peace to your family?
- How have you brought peace to your relationships with friends and strangers?

Standing Up for Peace

Share some examples or stories of people who stood up for peace. They can be a famous historical figure, like Gandhi, or someone you read about in the newspaper, perhaps even a teen in your community.

Make a commitment to take action for peace. Learn how to compromise. If we learn to find common ground and solve problems peacefully on a small scale, it can translate into the larger community.

Make a commitment to pray for peace. Look for every chance you get to pray for peace: when you hear a siren, when you walk by a gun store, when you see violence reported in the newspaper, when you see kids arguing at school.

Jesus the Peacemaker

Jesus is the model peacemaker. Some of his followers wanted a king and warrior to liberate them, but Jesus wasn't a soldier or a fighter. He treated everyone with gentleness and compassion. He turned the other cheek when the Pharisees tried to goad him into an argument. He was forgiving others even as he died a violent death on the cross. His first words to the Apostles when he appeared to them after the resurrection were, "Peace be with you."

Closing

Jesus sets an example for us and calls us to work for peace with our friends, in our schools, in our communities, in our families, and in our world. That's why we hear at the end of Mass, "Go in peace to love and serve the Lord."

Pledge of Nonviolence

Making peace must start within ourselves, in our families, and in our parish. Each of us,

members of _____, commit ourselves to become
nonviolent and peaceable people:

To Respect Self and Others
To respect myself, to affirm others, and avoid uncaring criticism, hateful
words, physical attacks, and self-destructive behavior.

To Communicate Better
To share my feelings honestly, to look for safe ways to express my anger, and
to work at solving problems peacefully.

To Listen
To listen carefully to one another, especially those who disagree with me,
and to consider others' feelings and needs rather than insist on
having my own way.

To Forgive
To apologize and make amends when I have hurt another, to forgive
others, and to keep from holding grudges.

To Respect Nature
To treat the environment and all living things with respect and care.

To Recreate Nonviolently
To promote athletic and recreational activities that encourage
cooperation and to avoid activities that make violence look
exciting, funny, or acceptable.

To Be Courageous
To challenge violence in all its forms whenever I encounter it, whether
at home, at school, in the parish, or in the community, and to
stand with others who are treated unfairly.

Signed: _____ Date: _____

(The pledge is taken from the "Parish Pledge of Nonviolence" created by Families Against Violence Advocacy
Network, c/o Institute for Peace and Justice, found at *www.ipj-ppj.org/pledge.html*)

Resource 19

"I Would Rather Be Bread"

Reader 1: If you had your choice, which would you rather be?

Reader 2: Huh? Which would I rather be?

Reader 1: Yes. Would you rather be bread, or would you rather be a stone?

Reader 2: Oh, I guess I'd rather be bread.

Reader 1: Bread?

Reader 2: Right.

Reader 1: I'd rather be a stone. You can't build a house out of bread.

Reader 2: You can't build a family out of stones.

Reader 1: Stones are strong.

Reader 2: But bread, when it's shared, is even stronger. Did you ever share a stone?

Reader 1: What good is bread once it's shared? It's gone. And what have you got left? But with a stone . . .

Reader 2: What you've got left is . . . a stone.

Reader 1: At least you've got something.

Reader 2: I think I'd rather be bread.

Reader 1: If I asked you for a stone, would you give me bread?

Reader 2: If I asked you for bread, would you give me a stone?

Reader 1: You're not fair.

Reader 2: Hungry people would rather have bread.

Reader 1: But I'm not hungry.

Reader 2: So you'd rather be a stone.

Reader 1: I wouldn't want to be bread.

Reader 2: Hungry people would love you.

Reader 1: And then I'd be all used up.

Reader 2: But they wouldn't be hungry.

Reader 1: And I wouldn't *be!* Period!

Reader 2: But you are now?

Reader 1: I am what now?

Reader 2: You're *being?*

Reader 1: I'd rather be a stone.

Reader 2: I'd rather be bread.

Reader 1: Stones are good for sitting on.

Reader 2: Bread is good for sitting with.

Reader 1: Stones are good for throwing.

Reader 2: Bread is good for giving.

Reader 1: Stones are always the same—strong and solid. You can be secure like a rock.

Reader 2: Or cold like a stone.

Reader 1: Or stale like yesterday's bread.

Reader 2: Or useless like one in a million stones. I'd rather be bread.

Reader 1: I'd rather be a stone. Stones are good for making slippery ways rough.

Reader 2: And smooth lives bumpy. But bread can make a bumpy life smooth.

Reader 1: If you like breaded life.

Reader 2: Rather than stony living. Stones don't care.

Reader 1: And bread does?

Reader 2: When it's shared.

Reader 1: If I asked you for a stone, would you give me bread?

Reader 2: If I asked you for bread, would you give me a stone?

(This dialogue is adapted from "I Would Rather Be Bread" from *Vine & Branches,* vol. 2, by Maryann Hokowski, [Winona, MN: Saint Mary's Press, 1992], p. 47. Copyright © 1992 by Saint Mary's Press. All rights reserved.)

Suggestions for "Called to Celebrate Our Faith" Talk

This talk explores Jesus' call to celebrate our faith. You have about 15 minutes for this presentation. The following provides ideas and thought starters.

Scripture Passages

In your talk bring in at least one Scripture passage to illustrate how Jesus calls us to be peacemakers. The main passage to use is Acts 2:1–14, the story of Pentecost which is also the story of the birthday of the Church. Other passages you could consider are:

- Matt. 5:14–16—Don't put your lamp under a basket.
- 1 Cor. 10:31–33, 11:1—Do all for the glory of God.

We Need to Celebrate

Start your talk by telling some stories about your favorite family celebrations. What makes them so special? When something special happens, does your family celebrate by going out to dinner? Do you like to celebrate with your friends? What do you like to do?

Being Catholic Is Something Special

Have you ever been asked, "Why are you Catholic? What's so special about being Catholic?" Being Catholic is special because first of all it means we are followers of Jesus Christ, the King of Kings, and savior of the world! As Catholics we also have our Sacraments, the teaching of the Church, our commitment to the poor, and our love for God's word.

Being Catholic means that we are part of a universal Church. Somewhere in the world, at every minute of the day, there is someone some where celebrating Mass. Think of other examples you can share.

It isn't always easy being Catholic. We can be misunderstood, we can be put down by people of other faiths. We need to take courage from the Holy Spirit and stand up for what we believe.

Celebrating Our Faith

Many of our cultural celebrations, such as Christmas and Easter, are rooted in the Christian faith. Do we celebrate the real meaning of Christmas and Easter, or do we get caught up in the commercialism? We can celebrate our faith by making Christ the focal point of our Christmas and Easter celebrations.

On a personal level how do we celebrate our faith? Our lives are so busy, we hardly have time for our spiritual lives. Is a Sunday morning soccer game more important than God? Would we rather sleep in or go to Mass?

Here are some other ways we can celebrate our faith:

- Learn more about our faith so we can share it.
- We can participate actively in the Sacraments and in outreach in our community.
- We can go to Mass and receive Eucharist every week.
- We can get involved in the youth ministry.

Closing

We have a lot to celebrate about being Catholic, about being Christian. We each have different gifts and talents and we each can praise God in our own way.

Appendix A

Helpful Hints for Giving Talks

- Speak slowly and thoughtfully.
- Try to keep eye contact with your audience.
- Share examples and stories from your own life.
- Share your feelings; be open and honest.
- Use a Scripture passage, a song, or a poem to help make a point.
- Explore the use of symbols (for example, giving out a nail when inviting retreatants to join you on the way to the cross).
- Use humor if you are comfortable with it.
- Stay within your timeframe. Talks that are too short fail to challenge, and talks that are too long lose the attention of listeners.
- Stay on your topic. You may not need to hit all the points, but you need to meet the main theme of your talk.
- Give your talk to someone else before the retreat and ask for feedback.
- End with a question or a challenge for the retreatants; leave your audience with something on which to reflect.
- Most important, be yourself.

Appendix B

Guidelines for Retreat Team Leaders

Throughout the Retreat

1. Familiarize yourself with the retreat so you will be better able to clarify directions given by the retreat coordinator and other team members.
2. Participate in all activities and discussions on the retreat.
3. Help with giving out supplies and setting up for activities.
4. Follow all retreat ground rules and assist in enforcing these rules.
5. Set a good example by respecting and listening to the speakers.
6. Help all the retreatants feel welcome and comfortable.
7. Lead, encourage, affirm, support, and befriend the retreatants.

In Small Groups

8. Help each person in your small group get to know the others better.
9. If you have trouble getting things started, you could always begin with the person who, for example, has the next birthday, has the most letters in her or his last name, is wearing green, has a shirt with a sports logo on it, has the most siblings, and so on.
10. Be aware of the shy persons (who need more encouragement) and the rowdy ones (who need some calming down). It also helps to know if a young person is struggling with a loss or going through personal problems.
11. Keep to the given activity's topic and guide the discussion.
12. Contribute to, but do not dominate, the discussion.
13. Avoid yes or no questions that tend to shut down conversation. Instead, ask open-ended questions:
    - How do you feel?
    - What is your reaction to the talk?
    - What would you write for that question?
    - What do you think?
14. Do a lot of listening.
15. Make sure each person has a chance to contribute to the discussion; stress that each person's contribution is valuable.
16. Thank each person for her or his contribution.
17. Share your own responses, experiences, and ideas honestly and openly.
18. Don't be afraid to share your faith.

Appendix C

Index of Activities

Acknowledgments

(continued from page 4)

I wish to thank the following people for their support and assistance in preparing the programs in this book:

- My husband, Mike Murawski, and my children Maria, Kyrie, and David for their patience and time while I was writing this book.

- Michael Horace, Donna Meier and Donna Eisenbath, the youth retreat team at the Shrine of Our Lady of the Snows in Belleville, Illinois.

- The Youth Advisory Team of Holy Spirit Parish in Virginia Beach, Virginia: Teens: Anthony Afrisio, Nick and Adam Caton, Kelly Early, Marie Harmon, Andrew Hughes, Kasey Hudgins, Clarissa and Casie Laumann, Colleen Laurence, Jasmin Martinez, Laura Nnadi, Daniel Rosario, Christina and Rachel Theisen, Ellyse Zepeda, Mark Zito. Adults: Abby Causey, John Gallegos, Warren Martin, Robin Meyers, Paul Mowbray, Carol Ann Wright.

- All the young people and adults who come on retreat every year, offering ideas for new programs and ways to improve existing ones.

The song "Jesus, Remember Me" page 51; and song refrain / "Our darkness is never darkness . . ."; song 2 refrain, "Stay with me, remain . . ."; song 3 refrain, "Within our darkest night, . . ."; song 4 refrain, "By your cross and all the wounds . . ."; song 5 refrain "Bless the Lord, my soul, . . ."; and song 6 refrain, and "Wait for the Lord . . ." on page 62 are adapted from *Taizé: Songs for Prayer'* music: Jacques Berthier (1923–1994) (Chicago, IL: GIA Publications, Inc., 1998). Copyright © 1998 by Ateliers et Presses de Taizé, #71250 Taizé Community, (France) International Copyright Secured. All rights reserved. Used with permission.

The responsive prayer on page 55 is from the "Responsorial Psalm" PS. 91:1–2, 10–11, 12–13, 14–15 taken from the *Lectionary for Mass for Use in the Dioceses of the United States of America, second typical edition,* (New York: Catholic Book Publishing Company, 1970), page 48. Copyright © 1998, 1997, 1970, by the Confraternity of Christian Doctrine, Inc. Washington, DC. Used with permission. All rights reserved. No portion of this text may be reproduced by any means without permission in writing from the copyright owner.

The song's verses to "Were You There?" no. 160, page 56 are adapted from *Breaking Bread, 2003,* (Portland, OR: OPC Publications, 2002). Copyright © 2002 by Oregon Catholic Press. All rights reserved.

The extract "Joseph of Arimathea," page 63 is from *We Were There, A Way of the Cross* by Sarah A. O'Malley and Robert D. Eimer (Collegeville, MN: Liturgical Press, 1996), page 37. Copyright © 1996 by The Order of St. Benedict, Inc., Collegeville, Minnesota. All rights reserved. Used with permission.

The extract "Magdalene," pages 63–64 is from *Journey of Decision, A Way of the Cross* by Sarah A. O'Malley and Robert D. Eimer (Collegeville, MN: Liturgical Press, 1991), pages 30–31. Copyright © 1991 by The Order of St. Benedict, Inc., Collegeville, Minnesota. All rights reserved. Used with permission.

The activity on page 78 is adapted from the activity "Sponge Reflection" from *Vine & Branches,* vol. 3, by Maryann Hakowski (Winona, MN: Saint Mary's Press, 1994), pages 44–45. Copyright © 1994 by Saint Mary's Press. All rights reserved.

The prayer, Reading 2, page 83 was written by Mandy White, Pomona Catholic High School, Pomona, CA, from *Dreams Alive,* edited by Carl Koch (Winona, MN: Saint Mary's Press, 1991), page 30. Copyright © 1991 by Saint Mary's Press. All rights reserved.

On Handout 6 "The Magnificat Prayer" on page 99 is from *The Catholic Youth Bible,* New Revised Standard Version: Catholic Edition, edited by Brian Singer-Towns (Winona, MN: Saint Mary's Press, 2000), page 1200. Copyright © 2000 by Saint Mary's Press. All rights reserved.

The activity on page 116 is adapted from *Growing With Jesus,* by Maryann Hakowski (Notre Dame, IN: Ave Maria Press, 1993), pages 36–37. Copyright © 1993 by Ave Maria Press. All rights reserved.

The activity on page 120 is adapted from the activity "Human Knots" found in *Vine & Branches,* vol. 1, by Maryann Hakowski (Winona, MN: Saint Mary's Press, 1992), page 103. Copyright © 1992 by Saint Mary's Press. All rights reserved.

Handout 8 "Parish Pledge of Nonviolence" on page 140 is a pledge taken from the Families Against Violence Advocacy Network, c/o Institute for Peace and Justice, St. Louis, MO, found at *www.ipj-ppj.org/pledge.html*

Resource 19 "I Would Rather Be Bread" on page 122 is adapted from *Vine & Branches,* vol. 2, by Maryann Hakowski (Winona, MN: Saint Mary's Press, 1992), page 47. Copyright © 1992 by Saint Mary's Press. All rights reserved.

To view copyright terms and conditions for Internet materials cited here, log on to the home pages for the referenced Web sites.

During this book's preparation, all citations, facts, figures, names, addresses, telephone numbers, Internet URLs, and other information cited within were verified for accuracy. The authors and Saint Mary's Press staff have made every attempt to reference current and valid sources, but we cannot guarantee the content of any source, and we are not responsible for any changes that may have occurred since our verification. If you find an error in, or have a question or concern about, any of the information or sources listed within, please contact Saint Mary's Press. We strongly urge adults to monitor children's use of the Internet and other resources.

Other resources from Maryann Hakowski published by Saint Mary's Press:

Pathways to Praying With Teens

Prayer Ways

Scripture Walk Junior High: Bible Themes

Sharing the Sunday Scriptures with Youth: Cycle A

Sharing the Sunday Scriptures with Youth: Cycle B

Sharing the Sunday Scriptures with Youth: Cycle C

Vine & Branches 1: Resources for Youth Retreats

Vine & Branches 2: Resources for Youth Retreats

Vine & Branches 3: Resources for Youth Retreats